Fuzzy Management Methods

Series Editors
Andreas Meier, Fribourg, Switzerland
Witold Pedrycz, Edmonton, Canada
Edy Portmann, Bern, Switzerland

With today's information overload, it has become increasingly difficult to analyze the huge amounts of data and to generate appropriate management decisions. Furthermore, the data are often imprecise and will include both quantitative and qualitative elements. For these reasons it is important to extend traditional decision making processes by adding intuitive reasoning, human subjectivity and imprecision. To deal with uncertainty, vagueness, and imprecision, Lotfi A. Zadeh introduced fuzzy sets and fuzzy logic. In this book series "Fuzzy Management Methods" fuzzy logic is applied to extend portfolio analysis, scoring methods, customer relationship management, performance measurement, web reputation, web analytics and controlling, community marketing and other business domains to improve managerial decisions. Thus, fuzzy logic can be seen as a management method where appropriate concepts, software tools and languages build a powerful instrument for analyzing and controlling the business.

Aigul Kaskina

Citizen Privacy Framework

Case of a Fuzzy-based Recommender System
for Political Participation

Springer

Aigul Kaskina
Department of Informatics
University of Fribourg
Fribourg, Switzerland

ISSN 2196-4130   ISSN 2196-4149   (electronic)
Fuzzy Management Methods
ISBN 978-3-031-06023-6   ISBN 978-3-031-06021-2   (eBook)
https://doi.org/10.1007/978-3-031-06021-2

This Springer imprint is published by the registered company Springer Nature Switzerland AG
The registered company address is: Gewerbestrasse 11, 6330 Cham, Switzerland

*To my parents and Andreas Meier in
recognition of their support.*

Foreword

Privacy has become an increasingly relevant topic in the field of social information systems, and particularly in the field of eDemocracy, where applications increasingly gather tremendous amounts of user data as input to the democratic process, for political discussion, or for recommendation purposes. This data may pose a severe threat to user privacy, for example, if accessed by untrusted parties, or used inappropriately. In essence, users of these systems face a vexing tradeoff: disclosing their information would increase their ability to participate in the online discourse that these systems enable, but privacy concerns urge them to refrain from sharing more than a nominal amount of information with these systems.

As people vary substantially with regard to how they value this tradeoff, privacy advocates suggest giving users an informed choice regarding the disclosure and use of their personal information. Unfortunately, the privacy implications of most modern information systems are so complex that even the most motivated users are unable to take effective control over their privacy settings without reaching the limits of their cognitive abilities. To overcome these problems, researchers are increasingly focusing on *user-tailored privacy* as a means to provide personalized privacy decision support. Broadly speaking, user-tailored privacy first creates a user model based on a contextualized understanding of users' privacy behaviors and then uses this model to adapt the default privacy settings, privacy notices, the privacy-setting interface, and/or the personalization mechanism to each individual user's preferences.

The academic understanding of user models for privacy has evolved from unidimensional to multidimensional to profile-based models. In most systems, however, the privacy preferences of users are complex and varied to an extent that they cannot be captured in a small discrete set of profiles. This is the central observation upon which Dr. Aigul Kaskina based her thesis *A Fuzzy-Based User Privacy Framework and Recommender System: Case of a Platform for Political Participation*, which is published in this book and for which she received her PhD in 2018 from the Faculty of Science at the University of Fribourg in Switzerland. Dr. Kaskina's work proposes *fuzzy clustering* as a much-needed solution to this problem, since it serves as a compromise between the simplicity and elegance of simple profiles and the advanced ability to capture each individual user's privacy preferences of recommendation approaches such as collaborative filtering.

While the broader goal of this book is to develop a conceptual framework that enhances citizens' privacy in eDemocracy by generating personalized privacy recommendations, it can primarily be commended for its direct, real-life application of user-tailored privacy in *ParticipaIntelligente*, an online political participation platform in Ecuador. Although political discourse is more fruitful in audience-restricted environments, the user study presented in this book finds substantial amount of variation in the privacy settings of 391 users of this application. In fact, many of these users do not restrict the visibility of their contributions and interactions on the platform, most likely because of a lack of knowledge and/or engagement. To help these users, Dr. Kaskina implements a fuzzy-based privacy recommender, which analyzes the user's current privacy settings and provides a recommendation for "better" settings. Effectively, this system leverages the efforts of users who possess sufficient knowledge and motivation to spend effort to set their privacy settings to provide personalized recommendations to users who do not possess such knowledge or motivation. The accuracy of multiple clustering methods and cluster granularities is considered, and the book culminates in a user-centric comparison of "sharp" (on average much different from users' own settings) and "soft" (not too different from users' own profiles) recommendation approaches against users' manually selected settings. Particularly, the "soft" recommendations result in lower reactance but also a somewhat lower outcome satisfaction, while the "sharp" recommendations score equal to users' own settings on outcome satisfaction but perform worse on all other metrics.

To conclude, this book contains trailblazing work in the use of fuzzy clustering for privacy preference prediction. I strongly recommend this book to user modeling researchers interested in a practical application of fuzzy clustering, to privacy researchers interested in the state of the art in privacy modeling, and to system designers and service providers in eDemocracy who want to learn about ways to build systems that respect the privacy of their users.

School of Computing   Dr. Bart P. Knijnenburg
Clemson University
United States of America

Acknowledgments

ego curious, ergo sum. je suis curieux, donc je suis

I would like to acknowledge the immense support from my supervisor, Prof Dr Andreas Meier, who helped make this thesis feasible. Thank you, Andreas, for supporting me in developing my capabilities as an independent researcher. This work was another step on the way of discovering and finding myself. I was also surrounded with the continuous support and mentoring from my dear colleagues Luis Teran, Marcel Wehrle, Alexander Denzler, Dac Hoa and others, for which I am extremely grateful. Your valuable advice encouraged me to move further. A special thank you goes to Luis Teran and Marcel Wehrle for their technical support during the research project. A valuable engagement from Bart Knijnenburg and Edy Portmann profoundly contributed to the accomplishment of the thesis. Your great expertise and scientific enthusiasm was incredibly inspiring and shaped my research mind. Thank you for your support and insightful collaboration. It was also a pleasure to collaborate with outstanding students Nevena Radovanovic, Sonia Parani and Luka Hamza. Thank you for working on common projects where I have learned new things since working with you. To Sylviane Pilloud and Elisabeth Brügger, I give a sincere thank you for helping me during my stay and the teaching activities at the University of Fribourg. I am glad to have met my friends with whom I have enjoyed these 4 years of research, in particular, Lorena Recalde, Ximena Jativa Sierra, Marco Schneiter, Liza Zimmerman, Melanie Boninsegni, Minh Tue Nguyen, Reza Ghaiumy Anaraky and other dear friends from all over the world. Finally, an endless gratitude and love to my parents for bringing me into this beautiful world.

Contents

List of Figures

List of Tables

List of Acronyms

APE	Absolute Percent Error
CE	Classification Error
CFA	Confirmatory Factor Analysis
CPP	Citizens Privacy Profile
CS	Crisp Silhouette
FCM	Fuzzy C-means Algorithm
FS	Fuzzy Silhouette
IRT	Item Response Theory
KNN	k-Nearest Neighbour Algorithm
MAE	Mean Absolute Error
MPC	Modified Partition Coefficient
MSE	Mean Square Error
OS	Outcome Satisfaction
OSA	Objective System Aspects
PAM	Partitioning Around Medoids
PBC	Privacy Behaviour Consistency
PC	Partition Coefficient
PE	Partition Entropy
PI	ParticipaInteligente
PRQ	Perceived Recommendation Quality
PSH	Perceived Recommendation Sharpness
PPA	Personalised Privacy Assistant
RMSE	Root Mean Square Error
SSA	Subjective System Aspect
UX	User Experience
VAAs	Voting Advice Applications
VAT	Visual Assessment of Cluster Tendency
WAM	Weighted Average Mean
XBI	Xie and Beni's Index

Chapter 1
Introduction

1.1 Motivation

Westin (1968) defined the individual's privacy right as when "each individual is continually engaged in a personal adjustment process in which he balances the desire for privacy with the desire for disclosure and communication of himself to others, in light of the environmental conditions and social norms set by the society in which he lives". After five decades this definition is a still vivid reality. However, the major difference nowadays is that social norms are set by digital societies, where the personal desire for disclosure can be expressed via privacy controls as designed by online service providers.

Moreover, a human's preferences are often ill-defined (Bettman et al., 1998), as is their ability to navigate the risks and benefits of information disclosure in different contexts. In the digitalised world every piece of personal information might become sensitive information. On the one hand, there are plenty of online information systems ready to collect citizens' personal data, however, on the other, citizens, though having control over their personal information, are increasingly exposing their data. This relates to the control paradox which shows that more online control for privacy makes people more likely to reveal information about themselves (Brandimarte et al., 2013).

Even if people are stating that they want privacy, their actions are saying otherwise. Such inconsistent behaviour is termed as privacy paradox (Norberg et al., 2007). People can easily give up their personal data, for instance, for the alimentary rewards by neglecting associated privacy risks. People seem to lack concern with privacy, until receiving an appropriate notice. Technology services might take advantages of such low privacy-aware behaviour of users: unprecedented collection of data (e.g., cell-phone location, click-streams, credit card use, etc.), selling this data to entities interested in obtaining this information. Considering the complicated human's privacy decision-making nature, the motivation of this thesis focuses on the analysis of people's privacy behaviour in the context of online

A. Kaskina, *Citizen Privacy Framework*, Fuzzy Management Methods, https://doi.org/10.1007/978-3-031-06021-2_1

political platform, in particular, how to quantify their privacy attitudes and how to generate privacy settings recommendations which might positively impact their future desire for disclosure.

1.2 Objectives

To address these listed issues, this book proposes an information system design that supports citizens to regulate their privacy boundaries in the online environment for political participation. The objective of this Ph.D. research aims at developing a conceptual framework and intelligent engine that enhances citizens' privacy in e-Democracy application by generating personalised privacy recommendations. The application of fuzzy logic techniques is proposed in order to facilitate the accuracy and utility of intelligent privacy recommendations.

1.3 Research Questions

In this section, a number of research questions are presented that provide an overview of the goals and scope of this book. The motivation relevant to each research question and the methods applied are discussed below.

In order to measure people's privacy attitudes and other factors that influence their desire of disclosure it is important to define a measurement privacy framework within a chosen application context. Therefore, the first research question is: "*RQ1. How can a user privacy profile be designed on a platform for political participation?*". Several research methods were used to answer this question. First, through an extensive *literature review* approach, the critical points of the current knowledge, theoretical and methodological recommendations are reviewed (see Chap. 2). Second, to explicate a design of the preferred information system, *a conceptual framework* is presented (see Chap. 3).

The analysis of users' disclosure tendencies and their privacy decision-making depends on the chosen quantification tools. This thesis proposed an alternative approach for classification of people's privacy preferences by means of fuzzy clustering which have been applied for the first time in the existing research field. Thus, the second research question addresses: "*RQ2. How do fuzzy clustering techniques unveil users' disclosure behaviour on a political platform?*". As application field of privacy issues is broad enough (e.g., health-, insurance-, education-, etc. related privacy), the application of the *case study* method is relevant in this thesis. *The case study* research method provides an in-depth investigation of the focal context, individual, group or event. This thesis addresses the online political participation context of the citizens of Ecuador using an online platform called the Participa

Inteligente[1] during presidential elections period. In addition, having the models of user privacy preferences build upon fuzzy clustering, the following user privacy-decision support is regarded as the next research question of the thesis: *"RQ3. How can an architecture for a fuzzy-based recommender system for privacy settings be designed?"*. For this question, the *prototyping* method was applied as a basis for the proof of the proposed conceptual framework.

There are many solutions exist to solve the aforementioned motivation of this research. The success of the proposed solution depends not only on its distinctive advantages but also on the kind of limitations that follow with implementation of such a solution. With this in mind, the fourth research question is: *"RQ4. What are the advantages and disadvantages of applying fuzzy-based approaches in user privacy decision-making?"*. To answer this question the evaluation methods in a form of a structured interviews are conducted. In particular, a *user-centric evaluation* approach is developed to answer the aforementioned question. The statistical analysis provides the quantitative interpretation of the collected dataset during this evaluation, and relevant conclusions are derived.

1.4   Research Methods

In alignment with defined research questions and perspective research methods, the general methodology of the entire book is based on the design science research approach proposed by Von Alan et al. (2004). Figure 1.1 displays the general research framework of the design science approach adapted for the undertaken research of this book. The advantageous characteristic of the research using design science approach is that the research outcome (artefacts) provides contribution not only to the application of the knowledge base (add-on to the theory) but also to the application in the appropriate environment (add-on solution to the practical issue). Von Alan et al. (2004) stated that the design science intends to solve identified organisational problems through creation and evaluation of IT artefacts. The kind of artefacts may be represented as constructs, models, methods and instantiations. To that, this research aimed to produce two artefacts: the first artefact—*a citizen privacy profile framework* in a form of a model (see Chap. 3, Sect. 3.1.2) and the second artefact—*a fuzzy-based privacy recommender system prototype* in a form of a construct (see Chap. 4, Sect. 4.1.2), and a web-based application (see Chap. 4, Sect. 4.2). The research of this thesis lies in the field of information systems (IS) which is an applied research discipline. The theories of other disciplines, for instance, economics, computer science and social sciences, are often combined in an IS discipline to solve problems at the intersection of information technology and organisation (Peffers et al., 2007).

---

[1] https://participacioninteligente.org/.

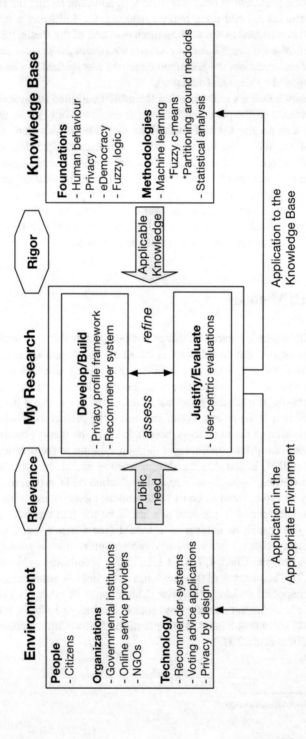

Fig. 1.1 Adapted framework of the Ph.D. research (adapted from Von Alan et al., 2004)

1.5   Thesis Outline

This thesis is organised into five chapters, with each chapter containing different sections. Following the introduction, the second chapter provides an in-depth literature background; the third is dedicated to the citizen's privacy profile framework; the forth describes the implementation of fuzzy-based privacy settings recommender system; and, finally, the fifth chapter summarises concluding remarks and future outlooks.

Chapter 2—Insights into Privacy Research This chapter introduces privacy as a concept based on the existing body of research. By presenting privacy as a paradoxical concept with underlying reasons for that, this chapter further reviews researchers' attempts to frame privacy within behavioural economic theory considering the user as a rational human. Reaching beyond the limits of user's decision-making rationality, the chapter then discusses the human cognition factors involved during the user privacy decision-making process. Finally, the chapter outlines existing research communities that are engaged with research projects that focus on privacy enhancing technologies.

Chapter 3—Citizen Privacy Profile Framework This chapter is dedicated to the conceptual framework of this book. Based on the extensive literature review, the chapter demonstrates a derived conceptual model of the existing research and placement of own contribution to the thesis. After, the conceptual framework of citizen privacy profile framework for Voting Advice Applications (VAAs) is introduced. Addressing the problem of privacy as an ambiguous and uncertain concept, this chapter promotes a possible importance and efficiency of using fuzzy logic in the development of privacy enhancing technologies. Thus, the implementation phases of the proposed citizen profile framework are presented. In particular, the development of the privacy management tool on the platform is described; the collection of the real-world dataset of user privacy profiles and analysis of the dataset structure is presented. User privacy profiles modelling is based on two different fuzzy clustering algorithms (fuzzy c-means, partitioning around medoids). The validation of fuzzy clustering results are explained. The evaluation of users' privacy behaviour on the platform is discussed to understand if there was a privacy paradox effect, if users' actual behaviour diverges with initial privacy attitudes and what are the reasons of using default settings.

Chapter 4—Fuzzy-Based Privacy Settings Recommender System This chapter introduces the fuzzy-based privacy settings recommender system. Along with a system architecture, this chapter describes the algorithm for calculating privacy recommendations with different distance metrics. The evaluation of the accuracy of the proposed models have been presented. This chapter also discusses the user evaluation of privacy recommendations, showing to what extent privacy recommendations are adapted by users and if recommendations were found useful.

Chapter 5—Conclusions In this chapter, concluding remarks and limitations of the current research are discussed. Further suggestions for the future research directions are outlined.

1.6 Own Research Contribution

In this section, a summary of the technical contributions and the list of the papers published by the author of this dissertation are provided. These resources are all related to the motivation or a part of this thesis.

* Kaskina A. *Exploring nuances of user privacy preferences on a platform for political participation.* In this work, the fuzzy c-means algorithm was applied to demonstrate the multidimensionality and the existence of fuzzy user privacy profiles, where the user at once can be associated with different privacy behaviour classes. It is based on the collected real-world dataset of user privacy profiles from Participa Inteligente platform (Kaskina, 2018).
* Meier A., Kaskina A., Teran L. *Politische Partizipation—eSociety anders gedacht.* In this work, the authors discuss the pyramid of political participation, explain the process chain for eVoting and eElection and introduce a recommendation system for electronic voting and elections that uses fuzzy logic. The protection of citizens' privacy is regulated in a privacy setting framework. In addition, it will be shown how political controlling could be introduced and how public memory could be successively built up (Meier et al., 2018).
* Kaskina A. *Differentiated User Privacy Support in the Digital Society.* This work proposes the concept of the differentiated user privacy framework which utilises a fuzzy inference system to create adaptive support for digital citizens in their privacy decision-making processes. It further presents the implementation of the user privacy profile part for VAA in Ecuador, including the development of functionalities such as information disclosure; the social network management functionality; the sharing techniques (Kaskina, 2017).
* Recalde L. and Kaskina A. *Who is suitable to be followed back when you are a Twitter interested in Politics?* The degree of citizens participation and political involvement within democratic societies may vary from one person to another. Similarly, the diversity of political engagement of users might be observed in online platforms. This paper proposed a framework to identify the level of interest in politics of a Twitter user for further design of the following back recommender system (Recalde & Kaskina, 2017).
* Kaskina A. and Meier A. *Integrating privacy and trust in voting advice applications.* In this paper, the authors explored the multidimensionality of user privacy behaviours based on the present user profile privacy framework. The authors showed that the complexity of user privacy profiles is reflected in variance of privacy decision per different data item in accordance with an audience representative (Kaskina & Meier, 2016).

- *Kaskina A. and Radovanovic N. How to Build Trust-Aware Voting Advice Applications?* Voting advice applications (VAAs) are intelligent systems that provide personalised recommendations of a political candidate/party to a voter with regard to their political attitudes. The paper presents a trust-aware Voting Advice Application which aims to improve the recommendation accuracy and to facilitate voter's decision-making processes and enhance citizens' participation (Kaskina & Radovanovic, 2016).
- *Teran L. and Kaskina A. Enhancing voting advice applications with dynamic profiles.* This paper presents a research of recommender systems applied on e-Government, particularly as it is an extension of VAAs. The authors introduce the use of fuzzy profiles that include both static and dynamic components. The dynamic profile generation contains different elements, such as context-aware information and privacy and trust concerns of users in order to provide different types of output recommendations and visualisations. Then, the system architecture and a prototype implementation of the extended VAA platform are presented (Terán & Kaskina, 2016).

References

Bettman, J. R., Luce, M. F., & Payne, J. W. (1998). Constructive consumer choice processes. *Journal of Consumer Research, 25*(3), 187–217.

Brandimarte, L., Acquisti, A., & Loewenstein, G. (2013). Misplaced confidences: Privacy and the control paradox. *Social Psychological and Personality Science, 4*(3), 340–347.

Kaskina, A. (2017). Differentiated user privacy support in the digital society. In Portmann, E. (Eds.), *Wirtschaftsinformatik in Theorie und Praxis* (pp. 141–152). Wiesbaden: Springer Vieweg.

Kaskina, A. (2018). Exploring nuances of user privacy preferences on a platform for political participation. In *2018 International Conference on eDemocracy & eGovernment (ICEDEG)* (pp. 89–94). IEEE.

Kaskina, A., & Meier, A. (2016). Integrating privacy and trust in voting advice applications. In *Third International Conference on eDemocracy & eGovernment (ICEDEG)* (pp. 20–25). IEEE.

Kaskina, A., & Radovanovic, N. (2016). How to build trust-aware voting advice applications? In *International Conference on Electronic Government and the Information Systems Perspective* (pp. 48–61). Springer.

Meier, A., Kaskina, A., & Teran, L. (2018). Politische Partizipation–eSociety anders gedacht. *HMD Praxis der Wirtschaftsinformatik* (pp. 1–13).

Norberg, P. A., Horne, D. R., & Horne, D. A. (2007). The privacy paradox: Personal information disclosure intentions versus behaviors. *Journal of Consumer Affairs, 41*(1), 100–126.

Peffers, K., Tuunanen, T., Rothenberger, M. A., & Chatterjee, S. (2007). A design science research methodology for information systems research. *Journal of Management Information Systems, 24*(3), 45–77.

Recalde, L., & Kaskina, A. (2017). Who is suitable to be followed back when you are a twitter interested in politics? In *Proceedings of the 18th Annual International Conference on Digital Government Research* (pp. 94–99). ACM.

Terán, L., & Kaskina, A. (2016). Enhancing voting advice applications with dynamic profiles. In *Proceedings of the 9th International Conference on Theory and Practice of Electronic Governance* (pp. 254–257). ACM.

Von Alan, R. H., March, S. T., Park, J., & Ram, S. (2004). Design science in information systems research. *MIS Quarterly, 28*(1), 75–105.

Westin, A. F. (1968). Privacy and freedom. *Washington and Lee Law Review, 25*(1), 166.

Chapter 2
Insights into Privacy Research

2.1 Economics of Privacy—a Rational Human

2.1.1 Privacy Calculus

Solove (2006) states that privacy cannot be considered independently from society, as "a need for privacy is a socially created need". Privacy is a challenging, vague and multifaceted concept, however, for decades researchers from social, psychological and computer science disciplines were focused on various aspects of privacy interpretation and conceptualisation. Altman (1977) tackles privacy as behavioural mechanisms used to regulate desired levels of privacy that occurs in all cultures. Altman defines privacy functions as: management of social interaction; establishment of plans and strategies for interacting with others; and development and maintenance of self-identity.

Palen and Dourish (2003) develop further Altman's understanding of privacy as a dialectic and dynamic boundary regulation process in the context of evolved information technologies. The authors propose a characterisation of privacy management scoped by three types of boundaries: the disclosure boundary that determines tensions between privacy and publicity; maintenance of self-identity; and temporality of boundaries defining the past, present and future interpretation of the disclosed information that could be in tension. It is upon the individual's decision to what extent the desired level of privacy is maintained.

Laufer and Wolfe (1977) present a privacy calculus behaviour outlined into three aspects: "individuals may engage in various behaviours believing that they can manage the information in new and later situations and thus minimise the potential consequences; individuals may simply not do certain things because the ability to manage the information at some later, even distant, point is unpredictable, or because even at the present moment the publicness or privateness of the act is ambiguously defined; the calculus of behaviour is related to the emergence of new technologies and the stage of the life cycle". Such interpretation of privacy

A. Kaskina, *Citizen Privacy Framework*, Fuzzy Management Methods,
https://doi.org/10.1007/978-3-031-06021-2_2

calculus evolves from the author's conceptualisation of privacy dimensions. Laufer and Wolfe (1977) base privacy on the situationality of the socio-historic environment in which the person grows over time throughout her life cycle.

Posner (1978) addresses privacy from a simple economic theory perspective where he defines two economic goods: "privacy" which is associated with information and facts about people that will incur costs to the information owner in order to withhold it; and "prying" related to people who are interested in other's people information which will also incur costs in order to discover it. The disclosure of one's information, according to Posner, is operated as transaction costs and, depending on the nature of the source of information, the costs may vary. By providing several examples of privacy as a good, and disclosure act as a transaction cost within individual's right of privacy, Posner, however, supports organisational privacy as, according to him, it has a greater economical impact rather than personal privacy.

Decades after, Acquisti and Grossklags (2005) also interpret people's privacy attitudes and behaviours through the lens of economic theories. The authors state that during privacy decision-making people's minds are framed with bounded rationality which is accompanied by situational externalities, information asymmetries, risks and uncertainties. The authors refer to the economical concept of "time inconsistent discounting", placing an example when an individual can easily fall for an instant low reward (short-term estimation) by disclosing some information without considering potential future negative implications (long-term estimation) of such disclosure. People are willing to act according to their own privacy interests, but due to complexity of privacy benefit/costs calculations, people naturally need to use simpler models that, ultimately, appear to be less beneficial for them.

Considering privacy through the lens of economic terms and privacy calculus leads to a capitalistic attitude towards one's privacy where businesses will excel at their best to motivate individuals to disclose as much information as possible. However, using simplistic benefits and costs model to target the best match of people's privacy attitudes and behaviours will not be enough. The privacy is not only complex in obtaining rational decision-making calculations but also bundled with psychological, cognitive and contextual cues. Thus, the critics of the economic view of privacy is discussed in the following section.

2.1.2   Death to Privacy Calculus?

Acquisti and Grossklags (2005) mention a "notice and choice" approach applied to establish benefits/costs relationships between customers and businesses. Sloan and Warner (2014) explain that the *notice* is a presentation of a business' terms (privacy policy or terms of use agreement), while the *choice* is an action signifying acceptance of these terms (clicking on an "I agree" button or proceeding using the website). Although being widely spread for several decades as an underlying mechanism for information protection and privacy self-management, the "notice and choice" approach is heavily criticised.

Hull (2015) argues that people are unable to make rational choices, where notice and choice strategy fails to provide a legible explanation of the privacy value. Economical perception of privacy treats it as a product, thus, increasing the privacy consumerism and neglecting a more social understanding of privacy. Hull (2015) proposes to understand privacy-protective behaviour as a form of resistance and of an effort "to refuse what we are" against those who have the power to impinge over our privacy. However, he points out that privacy self-management is mostly considered not as a resistance towards one's privacy preservation but treats preservation control as a "commercial transaction", and then considers this transactions as an expression of "consumer preferences". Thus, "the privacy self-management model obscures a social struggle, repackaging it as a well-functioning market".

Moreover, Solove (2013) encourages researchers, policy and law makers to start looking beyond the privacy self-management and to focus on consent dilemma. In particular, Solove highlights that any privacy self-management solution must confront a complex dilemma with consent. He draws attention to two main aspects that fail to make better use of privacy self-management solutions: *cognitive* and *structural* problems. The former one concerns the challenges on how humans make privacy decisions, fostered by the problem of uninformed individuals and further reinforced by the skewed decision-making. The latter addresses the structure of the privacy self-management tools that impedes its own goal of giving meaningful control over users' data.

In his paper "Death to privacy calculus?", Knijnenburg et al. (2017) pose under the question the practicality and ethicality of privacy calculus. The authors highlight that the contextualised anticipatory nature of privacy is far too complex to be handled solely upon privacy calculus, and that notice and choice together with privacy nudging, though being justifiable and ethical solutions, shortfall in providing enough protection. The authors propose a user-tailored privacy by design approach where the model of risk-benefit is a central part that consider which variables to include to sufficiently address the context. In that way, the system provides an automated support for users' privacy decision-making. Although the automation simplifies users' privacy decisions, one should not neglect if the model's trade-off is compensatory or not, which again can lead to the Hull's argument of the privacy consumerism.

2.1.3 Privacy Paradox

The gap between privacy attitude and actual disclosure behaviour is influenced by different types of rewards and benefits. In this vein, Hui et al. (2006) have studied several types of benefits and factors that motivate users to disclose their personal information. They outline seven types of benefits, categorised into extrinsic and intrinsic types, and investigate how those types of motivators can influence users to disclose more or less information. Hui et al. (2006) indicate that aside from the popular extrinsic benefits such as monetary saving or time saving benefits, various types of intrinsic benefits, such as social adjustment, novelty or altruism, when used appropriately, can also motivate users to engage in online disclosure.

The disclosure behaviour can differ between individuals depending on their respective personal motives. Nevertheless, people tend to show similar disclosure tendencies to each other. An interesting inclination in people's privacy behaviour has been presented in Norberg et al. (2007). "Privacy paradox" stated to be a disclosure behaviour when people's intention to limit their disclosure fades away at their effectuated disclosure act. Norberg et al. (2007) hypothesise that the gap between intentional and actual disclosure behaviour is product of two factors: it is a *risk* that, at first, substantially influences the individual's intention to disclose, while at the end it is a *trust* factor that significantly influences the individual's actual disclosure behaviour.

The existence of privacy paradox behaviour signals the departure from human-minded rationality. Compañó and Lusoli (2010) conducted a large scale online survey study among young Europeans in regard to perceptions and acceptance of risks, general motivations, attitudes and behaviours concerning electronic identity. Their study highlights the prevalence of privacy paradox where people with high perception of privacy risks still disclosed a range of personal information. The recent study by Athey et al. (2017) affirms the existence of the privacy paradox, discovered in a study where people's behaviour was observed in the digital (online information system) environment. The authors suggested that relying solely on disclosure behaviour can be misguiding. The results showed that despite stated privacy preferences, when given a small incentive the promised intentional disclosure disappears. Moreover, they found that additional effort costs seem to trigger the "laziness", so that users might fall back from their initial privacy-protective choices due to complexity and effort-demanding privacy controls.

In a digitalised world people are disclosing more and more personal information online. Besides the aforementioned concept of "privacy paradox", people are also confronted with various privacy compromises and trade-offs (e.g., "take it or leave it", "benefits and costs trade-off" and "privacy and personalisation trade-off"). With that, it becomes more difficult for people's minds to estimate implying risks in their disclosure behaviour. Moreover, one's privacy management strategies are not always effectively performed. For example, a non-user-friendly design of privacy controls presents to be a barrier for users in effectively maintaining their desired level of privacy (Johnson et al., 2012; Kelley et al., 2011b; Reinhardt et al., 2015; Watson et al., 2012).

2.2 Beyond Rationality—Human Cognition

2.2.1 Cognitive Heuristics Behind Disclosure Decisions

Why does recent research suggest viewing privacy beyond the rational mind and to step away from the economic interpretation of privacy decisions? Researchers are convinced that simplified economic models of benefits and costs produce a distorted reality regarding people's privacy attitudes. Problems of skewed disclosure decisions with involved cognitive, psychological heuristics affects a well-established utopia of having a rational user. That is a why a self-management approaches fail at the face of privacy paradox, as important underlying cognitive behaviours and biases are overlooked.

Lai and Hui (2006) suggest that framing questions in certain formats may unconsciously evoke higher levels of consumer participation. The authors discuss two default mechanisms, such as opt-in and opt-out, in the context of choice frame (e.g., "notify me about more health surveys") and rejection frame (e.g., "do not notify me about more health surveys"). The authors find that users with high privacy concerns experience positive and favourable attitudes towards participation in online activities when presented with the relevant choice frame.

Marmion et al. (2017) investigate which cognitive heuristics drive people while making disclosure decision and how it impacts their further behaviour. The authors apply credibility-framed heuristics which are divided into several classes (prominence, network, reliability, etc.) in a qualitative user study, by reporting results on how a particular heuristic has an impact on users' disclosure behaviour. For example, *network heuristic* shows that people tend to delegate their privacy decisions by relying on the recommendations of peers expecting others in conducting risk discovery for a particular disclosure decision. The authors conclude that instead of rational decision based on benefits and costs model, users are inclined to estimate trustworthiness based upon prominence and social network heuristics, relying on cues such as popularity, brand exposure or word of mouth which fundamentally lead to a "herd mentality".

Similarly, Gambino et al. (2016) find that in a moment of disclosure behaviour users form their decisions based on "interface-cue triggered cognitive heuristics". The authors outline several "positive heuristics" that encourage users to disclose their information as they supply the feeling of safety. As an example, *gatekeeping heuristic* invokes the sense of safety when the web services provides many layers of access (e.g., banking system with several steps of authorisation), and it mostly appeared in relation to sensitive data like banking, health information, etc. However, when appeared in less valuable websites like Facebook, multi-layers of access were deemed annoying. The authors also identify "negative heuristics" which, instead, inhibit users disclosure decisions lead by the distrust to a website. *intrusiveness heuristic* appears when users are provided with unsolicited items and, when users realise that their data has been used by third parties without their consent, it evokes a negative effect resulting in restraining their sharing behaviour.

Years prior, Camp (2009) stated that the lack of privacy-protective technologies adoption is partially due to ineffective risk communication arguing that "if naive users are unable to effectively evaluate their own risks and decisions, no amount of technology will be empowering for those users". The author draws attention to users tending to fail at understanding detailed risk communication which brings uncertainty. Consequently, users fall upon heuristics and biases in estimating risks. The use of mental models proved to be effective for uncertain decision-making in various domains. The author presents different situational cases (physical security, medical infection, economic failure, etc.) exposing security risk communications and what mental models appear to be present. Thus, the author concludes that mental models are more natural to people's mind in perceiving the risk, admitting that strictly rational approach is, in fact, irrational.

The argument in common drawn by the above-mentioned studies and others (Kang et al., 2015; Kehr et al., 2015; Sundar et al., 2013) is that the utopian assumption of a rational user capable of making privacy decision in uncertain environment is an illusion. The physical privacy is understood to be result of physical or tactical risk-avoidance behaviour, while online privacy is harder to understand, therefore, there is a greater uncertainty in decision-making (Camp, 2009). An unshaped definition of privacy and vague representation of implied risks and benefits do not permit users at their calculative skills make a rational decision, thus, leading to use cognitive abilities, such as heuristics, or to trigger psychological biases.

2.2.2   Enforced by Individual Characteristics?

The cognitive heuristics are not limited to psychological biases and perceptions. Individual characteristics are apparent to be complementary factors that influence people's disclosure behaviour. Demographical differences, personality peculiarities and social status, among others, are shown to explicate particular tendencies of people's privacy attitudes, intended and actual disclosure behaviour.

Cho et al. (2009) investigate individual characteristics and cultural factors that affect people's online privacy concerns and influence their further privacy protection behaviour. According to *individualism index (IND)*, based on Hofstede's framework, a person from individualistic countries tend to value the private life more than a someone from a collectivistic country where the intrusion of groups or an organisation is accepted. A study by Sawaya et al. (2017) supports the previous study and shows that Asian users (China, Japan, South Korea, etc.) are likely to exhibit less private behaviour online and to be less concerned with online privacy. In addition, Li et al. (2017) postulate that people from collectivistic countries (China, India, etc.) find it acceptable to disclose personal information to the government or employers as they tend to "subjugate individual rights and goals for a sense of commitment to the group and of self-sacrifice for the common good". In contrast, people from individualistic countries (US, Germany, etc.) deem such behaviour unacceptable as they feel less obligated to disclose personal information if there is no specific demand. They are more willing to disclose for paid services or for services with a pre-existing relationship to the service. With respect to gender characteristics, earlier studies indicate that female users tend to have higher privacy concerns and effectuate privacy-protective behaviours rather than their younger male equivalent (Cho et al., 2009; Lewis et al., 2008). However, a recent study shows that women self-disclose more than men on social networking site, for example, Facebook (Wang et al., 2016), while the study by Sawaya et al. (2017) indicates that there is no effect of gender on people's security behaviour. Also, this study reports that the income level has an effect, so that people with an income level of at least 60K (USD) per year have more diligent security behaviours when compared to those with an income lower than 60K (USD) per year.

For the individual's personality effect, early studies have investigated the relationship of personality and privacy preferences in offline environment. Marshall (1970) and Pedersen (1987) identified a highly similar set of privacy dimensions and described how personality determines peoples' privacy preferences. Marshall found a correlation between person's introversion and her total privacy score, while Pedersen highlighted that low self-esteem was associated with solitude and anonymity. Considering privacy disclosure in an online environment, Quercia et al. (2012), Ferwerda et al. (2016) using a Big Five personality measurement classified users and found that privacy conscious users are correlated with traits as openness and extraversion, and non-disclosure behaviour correlates with various personality characteristics depending on the data type. However, in their study Schrammel et al. (2009) reported that they could not find any significant relations between personality traits and information disclosure. In contrast, Egelman and Peer (2015) argued that personal traits, such as decision-making and risk-taking attitudes, are much stronger predictors for privacy attitudes than the traditional Big Five personality model.

Attempts undertaken by researchers to deconstruct the concept of privacy shows that the snowball composed of psychological and cognitive antecedents, individual differences and contextual cues, among others, makes it difficult to develop a universal framework. The main focus of this thesis lies in the argument heuristics in privacy decision-making must be accounted in the design of privacy profile frameworks and in automated privacy decisions support systems. This thesis makes a first attempt to address the cognitive nature of privacy decision-making by embedding fuzzy clustering approaches described later in the thesis.

2.3 Automating User Privacy Support

Due to the complexity of privacy controls it becomes problematic for people to precisely express their privacy preferences and estimate the potential risks of their disclosure behaviour. For example, Kelley et al. (2011a) found that users on Facebook are adapting their online behaviour to avoid the need to specify groups in the current Facebook interface. Whereas, in the case of Google+ circles, Watson et al. (2012) demonstrate that some participants still posted information with the expectation that the content could possibly be seen by anybody regardless of being able to share with a particular audience. To mitigate some of the existing privacy issues a *privacy by design* (PbD) regulation has been introduced by Cavoukian (2012). PbD is characterised by proactive measures to improve one's privacy. It suggests that privacy aspect of the information system should be embedded earlier in the design phase of the information system. Below, the overview of leading research institutions that undertake scientifically justified actions to support users' privacy in line with privacy by design approach is presented.

Carnegie Mellon University, USA *Usable privacy policy project*[1] focuses on addressing the problem of privacy policies which is usually left unread by users. This project aims to develop machine implementable standards and techniques that will help semi-automatically extract key privacy policy features from natural language website privacy policies. Further, these features are presented "to users in an easy-to-digest format that enables them to make more informed privacy decisions as they interact with different websites".

Berkley Laboratory for Usable and Experimental Security, USA[2] The goal of the research lab is to understand how users perceive various smartphone-related risks, their preferences for how their sensitive data should be used by third-party applications and the threat to the landscape. In addition, the research on web-based threats to privacy and security involves performing human subject experiments to examine how people respond to current mitigations, such as web browser security warnings and various privacy tools.

Clemson University, USA The *Privacy support for total learning architecture*[3] project applies user-tailored privacy by design which, in essence, predicts users' privacy preferences and behaviours and then provides adaptive nudges. In such personalised privacy decision support, machine learning techniques take over risk/benefit trade-off, context, users characteristics and other variables, so that decreasing users' decision burden over their privacy protection.

EPFL, Switzerland Researchers at EPFL developed *PriBot*—the first automated question-answering chatbot for privacy policies and *Polisis*—a unique way of visualising privacy policies. Using deep learning algorithms, these applications allows users to know what data the company is collecting and if it is shared with third parties, so that decreasing users' effort to read and understand the entire text of privacy policies.

---

[1] https://usableprivacy.org/.

[2] https://blues.cs.berkeley.edu/.

[3] https://www.researchgate.net/publication/316065621.

SOCIAM, England *The mobile app X-Ray* project aims to help end-users make better informed privacy decisions by making the hidden information flows within and behind social machines visible. In particular, Data Controller Indicators were developed that expose previously hidden information flows out of the web applications. Such indicators support people in making more confident and consistent choices, informed by the number and nature of third-party companies that access users' data (Van Kleek et al., 2017).

University of Fribourg, Switzerland The Ph.D. project titled *"A Fuzzy-Based User Privacy Framework and Recommender System: Case of a Platform for Political Participation"*. This project considers the Participa Inteligente's platform—a main function of which is to serve as a voting advice application. The aim is to develop privacy support for online citizens by using a combination of fuzzy clustering and recommender system techniques. Essentially, based on the real-world dataset from the citizens of Ecuador, the core of the proposed approach can be later applied within different cultural and application domains.

References

Acquisti, A., & Grossklags, J. (2005). Privacy and rationality in individual decision making. *IEEE Security & Privacy, 3*(1), 26–33.

Altman, I. (1977). Privacy regulation: Culturally universal or culturally specific? *Journal of Social Issues, 33*(3), 66–84.

Athey, S., Catalini, C., & Tucker, C. (2017). The digital privacy paradox: Small money, small costs, small talk. Technical report, National Bureau of Economic Research.

Camp, L. J. (2009). Mental models of privacy and security. *IEEE Technology and Society Magazine, 28*(3), 37–46.

Cavoukian, A. (2012). Privacy by design [leading edge]. *IEEE Technology and Society Magazine, 31*(4), 18–19.

Cho, H., Rivera-Sánchez, M., & Lim, S. S. (2009). A multinational study on online privacy: Global concerns and local responses. *New Media & Society, 11*(3), 395–416.

Compañó, R., & Lusoli, W. (2010). The policy maker's anguish: Regulating personal data behavior between paradoxes and dilemmas. In *Economics of Information Security and Privacy* (pp. 169–185). Springer.

Egelman, S., & Peer, E. (2015). Predicting privacy and security attitudes. *ACM SIGCAS Computers and Society, 45*(1), 22–28.

Ferwerda, B., Schedl, M., & Tkalcic, M. (2016). Personality traits and the relationship with (non-) disclosure behavior on Facebook. In *Proceedings of the 25th International Conference Companion on World Wide Web* (pp. 565–568). International World Wide Web Conferences Steering Committee.

Gambino, A., Kim, J., Sundar, S. S., Ge, J., & Rosson, M. B. (2016). User disbelief in privacy paradox: Heuristics that determine disclosure. In *Proceedings of the 2016 CHI Conference Extended Abstracts on Human Factors in Computing Systems* (pp. 2837–2843). ACM.

Hui, K., Tan, B., & Goh, C. (2006). Online information disclosure: Motivators and measurements. *ACM Transactions on Internet Technology, 6*(4), 415–441.

Hull, G. (2015). Successful failure: what Foucault can teach us about privacy self-management in a world of Facebook and big data. *Ethics and Information Technology, 17*(2), 89–101.

Johnson, M., Egelman, S., & Bellovin, S. M. (2012). Facebook and privacy: It's complicated. In *Proceedings of the Eighth Symposium on Usable Privacy and Security*.

Kang, R., Dabbish, L., Fruchter, N., & Kiesler, S. (2015). My data just goes everywhere? User mental models of the internet and implications for privacy and security. In *Symposium on Usable Privacy and Security (SOUPS)* (pp. 39–52). Berkeley, CA: USENIX Association.

Kehr, F., Wentzel, D., Kowatsch, T., & Fleisch, E. (2015). Rethinking privacy decisions: Pre-existing attitudes, pre-existing emotional states, and a situational privacy calculus. AIS.

Kelley, P., Brewer, R., Mayer, Y., Cranor, L. F., & Sadeh, N. (2011a). An investigation into Facebook friend grouping. In *IFIP Conference on Human-Computer Interaction* (pp. 216–233). Springer Berlin Heidelberg.

Kelley, P. G., Brewer, R., Mayer, Y., Cranor, L. F., & Sadeh, N. (2011b). An investigation into Facebook friend grouping. In *IFIP Conference on Human-Computer Interaction* (pp. 216–233). Springer.

Knijnenburg, B. P., Raybourn, E. M., Cherry, D., Wilkinson, D., Sivakumar, S., & Sloan, H. (2017). Death to the privacy calculus?

Lai, Y.-L., & Hui, K.-L. (2006). Internet opt-in and opt-out: Investigating the roles of frames, defaults and privacy concerns. In *Proceedings of the 2006 ACM SIGMIS CPR Conference on Computer Personnel Research: Forty Four Years of Computer Personnel Research: Achievements, Challenges & the Future* (pp. 253–263). ACM.

Laufer, R. S., & Wolfe, M. (1977). Privacy as a concept and a social issue: A multidimensional developmental theory. *Journal of social Issues, 33*(3), 22–42.

Lewis, K., Kaufman, J., & Christakis, N. (2008). The taste for privacy: An analysis of college student privacy settings in an online social network. *Journal of Computer-Mediated Communication, 14*(1), 79–100.

Li, Y., Kobsa, A., Knijnenburg, B. P., Nguyen, C., et al. (2017). Cross-cultural privacy prediction. *Proceedings on Privacy Enhancing Technologies, 2017*(2), 113–132.

Marmion, V., Bishop, F., Millard, D. E., & Stevenage, S. V. (2017). The cognitive heuristics behind disclosure decisions. In *International Conference on Social Informatics* (pp. 591–607). Springer.

Marshall, N. (1970). Personality correlates of orientation toward privacy. In *Proceedings of the 2nd Annual Environmental Design Research Association Conference* (pp. 316–319).

Norberg, P. A., Horne, D. R., & Horne, D. A. (2007). The privacy paradox: Personal information disclosure intentions versus behaviors. *Journal of Consumer Affairs, 41*(1), 100–126.

Palen, L., & Dourish, P. (2003). Unpacking privacy for a networked world. In *Proceedings of the SIGCHI Conference on Human Factors in Computing Systems*. ACM.

Pedersen, D. (1987). Relationship of personality to privacy preferences. *Journal of Social Behavior & Personality*.

Posner, R. A. (1978). Economic theory of privacy. *Regulation, 2*, 19.

Quercia, D., Casas, D. L., Pesce, J. P., Kosinski, M., Almeida, V., & Crowcroft, J. (2012). Facebook and privacy: The balancing act of personality, gender, and relationship currency. In *ICWSM*.

Reinhardt, D., Engelmann, F., & Hollick, M. (2015). Can I help you setting your privacy? A survey-based exploration of users' attitudes towards privacy suggestions. In *Proceedings of the 13th International Conference on Advances in Mobile Computing and Multimedia* (pp. 347–356). ACM.

Sawaya, Y., Sharif, M., Christin, N., Kubota, A., Nakarai, A., & Yamada, A. (2017). Self-confidence trumps knowledge: A cross-cultural study of security behavior. In *Proceedings of the 2017 CHI Conference on Human Factors in Computing Systems* (pp. 2202–2214). ACM.

Schrammel, J., Köffel, C., & Tscheligi, M. (2009). How much do you tell? Information disclosure behaviour indifferent types of online communities. In *Proceedings of the Fourth International Conference on Communities and Technologies* (pp. 275–284). ACM.

Sloan, R. H., & Warner, R. (2014). Beyond notice and choice: Privacy, norms, and consent. *Journal of High Technology Law, 14*, 370.

Solove, D. J. (2006). A taxonomy of privacy. *University of Pennsylvania Law Review, 154*(3), 477.

Solove, D. J. (2013). Privacy self-management and the consent dilemma. *Harvard Law Review, 126*, 1880.

Sundar, S. S., Kang, H., Wu, M., Go, E., & Zhang, B. (2013). Unlocking the privacy paradox: Do cognitive heuristics hold the key? In *CHI'13 Extended Abstracts on Human Factors in Computing Systems* (pp. 811–816). ACM.

Van Kleek, M., Liccardi, I., Binns, R., Zhao, J., Weitzner, D. J., & Shadbolt, N. (2017). Better the devil you know: Exposing the data sharing practices of smartphone apps. In *Proceedings of the 2017 CHI Conference on Human Factors in Computing Systems* (pp. 5208–5220). ACM.

Wang, Y.-C., Burke, M., & Kraut, R. (2016). Modeling self-disclosure in social networking sites. In *Proceedings of the 19th ACM Conference on Computer-Supported Cooperative Work & Social Computing* (pp. 74–85). ACM.

Watson, J., Besmer, A., & Lipford, H. (2012). + Your circles: Sharing behavior on Google +. In *Proceedings of the Eighth Symposium on Usable Privacy and Security* (p. 12). ACM.

Chapter 3
Citizen Privacy Profile Framework

3.1 Conceptual Development

3.1.1 Overview of Existing Privacy Frameworks

Grounded on the design science research process and the literature review of the existing body of knowledge, the current and own research contribution was framed into a model as displayed in Fig. 3.1. A broad research framework was developed that identified the critical variables for measurements derived from various and existing *privacy frameworks* (Aïmeur et al., 2009; Liu & Terzi, 2010). Once the privacy framework is defined, the subsequent step was to build *privacy profiles* (Kobsa, 2001) of users which, in earlier research, were quantified as *unidimensional profiles* (Westin, 1968). The first substantial improvement was achieved when researchers moved from "one-size fits all approach" and started to quantify privacy profiles across several dimensions—*multidimensional profiles* (Knijnenburg et al., 2013; Wisniewski et al., 2017). The fact that people's privacy attitudes may vary along different dimensions helps not only to differentiate between the implied context but also to improve the personalisation of people's privacy attitudes and preferences. Once privacy profiles are defined, users are assigned to *segmented* groups with the help of various machine learning techniques. This information is later used in the development of *smart privacy management tools* or *privacy-enhanced applications*. The former tools aim to assist users' personal privacy in the online environment, while the latter applications utilise users' privacy preferences to improve their own online services.

With regard to the contribution of this thesis, Fig. 3.1 indicates that profiling should move one step further towards the *fuzzy profiles* (Kaskina, 2018), which not only increases the accuracy of the user segmentation and personalisation but also assists in capturing user's cognitive perceptions of privacy. In turn, using a fuzzy logic approach, including computing with words, fuzzy clustering and fuzzy inference approach, among others, can significantly improve the segmentation

© The Author(s), under exclusive license to Springer Nature Switzerland AG 2022
A. Kaskina, *Citizen Privacy Framework*, Fuzzy Management Methods,
https://doi.org/10.1007/978-3-031-06021-2_3

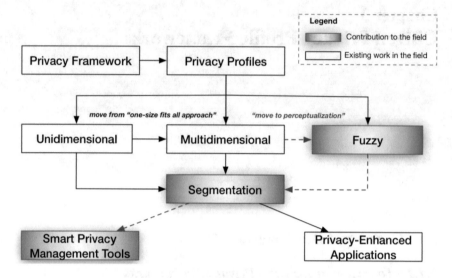

Fig. 3.1 Conceptual model of the existing research and own contribution

of privacy user groups and the development of smart privacy controls. In the following sections we discuss in detail some existing privacy frameworks and privacy management tools and then present the own privacy framework and fuzzy-based privacy recommender system in the context of political participation. Below we discuss the existing privacy frameworks addressed in the research domain. By analysing their advantages and disadvantages, we introduce our privacy framework designed for the voting advice application as mentioned in Sect. 3.1.2.

Liu et al. framework

Liu and Terzi (2010) proposed a framework that takes into account privacy settings of users with respect to their profile items. The framework computes privacy scores of users using Item Response Theory (IRT), thus, estimating their potential privacy risks. The authors mathematically defined the sensitivity of the profile item and the visibility parameter, which indicates how visible this item is to the social network of the user. As IRT methodology is primarily used in psychometrics, Liu and Terzi (2010) relate the examinee to a user and questions to profile items. The ability of the examinee is mapped to a user's privacy attitude, which is quantified by the level of the user's privacy concern. Thus, they indicate two types of users based on their privacy concerns: conservative/introverts and careless/extraverts. By grouping a set of users into groups based on their attitude types, they calculate the sensitivity and visibility of profile items by scoring their privacy risk.

Later, Munemasa and Iwaihara (2011) developed a visualisation tool of users' privacy setting tendencies. In their work the authors apply (Liu & Terzi, 2010) framework to evaluate the openness level of user profile by assigning privacy scores. In this way, every user profile openness was classified based on privacy score attitudes: introvert, extravert and the additional average attitude. To conclude, the proposed IRT-based privacy framework can have several disadvantages. The sensitivity parameter was quantified as a "difficulty parameter" which takes values from a negative to positive infinite range. Such interpretation of sensitivity is very uncertain and lacks the profile item context. Additionally, the attitude score calculation is based on the sensitive parameter using likelihood estimation. As a result, users' attitudes are represented as a score, and the framework implements one-dimensional clustering of users. Therefore, this framework is a demonstrative example where users' privacy is quantified as a unidimensional profile by ignoring the multi-level openness degrees (granularity of visibility) and downgrading the whole profile into one score.

Aimeur et al. Framework

To enable users to communicate their privacy preferences before allowing access to their data, Aïmeur et al. (2009) developed a privacy framework where users' privacy preferences can be configured in a form of a "user privacy policy". First, the framework considers users' privacy concerns that are grouped based on the security risk, reputation and credibility risk, profiling risk etc. Second, the authors also identify profile viewers (people to whom the data is disclosed) which are categorised into best friends, normal friends, casual friends and visitors. Third, the users' data is also classified into categories related to the security risks. Then, they derive users' privacy levels (No Privacy, Soft Privacy, Hard Privacy, Full Privacy) and tracking levels (Strong Tracking, Weak Tracking and No Tracking) using the predefined categorisation of the data, the user privacy concerns and profile viewers. Thus, by using "user privacy policy", the data owners can grant the access of the data only if the users, who request the access, follow their policy's conditions. In general, compared to previous work, Aïmeur et al. (2009) framework presents to be more contextualised. For example, user's privacy attitude (concern) quantification is based on several dimensions as well as profile viewers being categorised into definitive group types. However, both, privacy levels and tracking levels, were limited to a static configuration that cannot fully characterise each user's personal "taste" of privacy settings. To that, users are invited to configure the suitable privacy policy themselves. This is a drawback of this framework as it requires substantial user effort and time to conduct an extensive privacy calculus to perform their own configuration. Even though the framework aims to inform and facilitate one's privacy control, there is a possibility that, over time, the user might experience a significant "configuration fatigue".

Knijnenburg et al. Framework

Knijnenburg et al. (2013) argue that user privacy behaviour while disclosing personal information appears to have not just one "disclosure tendency", but several. Opposingly, the user privacy behaviour classification should move from the "one-size-fits-all" approach, thus, considering people's privacy behaviour per various dimensions. A multidimensional conceptualisation of privacy behaviours will not only provide a more robust measurement of users' privacy but also give more precise classification of groups of people, thus, supporting them to tailor their privacy. Based on these arguments, Knijnenburg (2017) presents a user-tailored privacy framework. This framework aims to shape out an optimal solution for users' privacy support by considering the multidimensional nature of people's privacy behaviours and contextual variables. It considers context-specific variables that focus on the context of the requested data, personal user's characteristics, features of the data recipients and other system-specific factors. Undoubtedly, this framework goes beyond simplified versions of privacy frameworks by proposing three steps for a personalised privacy: (1) measure user's privacy-related characteristics and behaviours, (2) use the output from the first step to build a user privacy model, and (3) adapt systems privacy settings according to inferred privacy preferences. One of the possible pitfalls of such a framework is that while capturing its optimality, the practical feasibility is weakly addressed. Even though it is contextually enriched, in a real-world scenario, it becomes more complicated to practically build such architectures. Thus, a potential drawback of this framework is a missing detailed specification of each part of the framework. In Sect. 4.1, we will discuss existing technical implementations of privacy frameworks which aim to provide an intelligent automated user privacy control.

3.1.2 Citizen Privacy Profile (CPP) Framework

To the best of our knowledge, none of the past studies focused on developing the privacy framework specifically to the needs of voting advice applications (VAAs). It is vital for political platforms, like VAAs, to be concerned with citizens' desire to position themselves on the platform with respect to their expressed privacy preferences. VAAs are heavily associated with a political context, where citizens may be exposed to various privacy risks. Those risks linked to the underlying context of politics may affect the disclosure behaviour strategies of users.

As an example, in their study, Huckfeldt and Sprague (1987) show that voters tend to be accurate in their perceptions of discussion partners who agree with their own preferences, e.g., Reagan voters tend to recognise other Reagan voters. This is especially the case when surrounding environment preferences are supportive of the voter's preferences. Reagan voters are more likely to perceive Mondale discussants accurately in Mondale surrounding contexts and less likely to perceive them accurately in Reagan surrounding contexts. Put differently, members of the political minority accurately perceive members of the majority, while members of the majority do not accurately perceive members of the minority (Huckfeldt & Sprague, 1987). This behaviour can advise the need of the system functionality to create groups on the platform which can provide the opportunity for private discussions among users with similar political views.

An exposure to diverse political views within political discussion networks does not necessarily enhance political communication activities. According to Kwon et al. (2015), being exposed to varied political opinions may induce an uncertainty in one's own political beliefs, leading them to hesitancy to publicly claim their political positions, thus avoiding political participation. However, the study of Kim (2011) manifests that those people who actively use social networking sites and active on online political messaging are mostly those who faced to cross-cutting political discussion, i.e., political difference. This theoretical background can inform the design of citizen privacy profile framework; in particular, the design of the functionality that will allow to disclose or to hide user's political opinions which will facilitate to manage one's relations within her social network and by personal volition to avoid or engage in the diverse political discussions.

Voting Advice Applications

In the field of e-Democracy, the emerging tools called voting advice applications (VAAs) are gaining great interest among researchers as well as among citizens. The core aim of VAAs is to facilitate decision-making processes of citizens and enhance their participation in e-Democracy. In essence, VAAs are designed to help voters to choose a party or a candidate during political election campaigns. Voters are creating their political profiles, and by comparing them with profiles of nominated candidates/parties, using different statistical methods, the system recommends which candidate's/party's political view is the closest to the political view of the voter. In recent years, these applications have been heavily used during the election period in the European countries (Garzia & Marschall, 2012).

In the technical perspective, recommender techniques applied in VAAs usually use distance measure between candidate and voter profiles, or collaborative filtering, and in some applications model-based approach. However, mentioned techniques are limited as the data can be inferred only from the policy-issues statements. The first attempt of VAAs extensions with social elements is proposed by Katakis et al. (2014), which includes a friend function or blogs that solely enable interactions between users, while the generated datum from these functions remains unused. However, this datum can improve the accuracy of the recommendation computation. Kaskina and Radovanovic (2016) proposed a trust-aware VAAs, which aimed to improve the recommendation accuracy by establishing the candidates-to-voters communication via the forum channel. The candidates' reputation scores based on their behaviour on the forum are included into the calculation of the similarity of political profiles between voters and candidates.

In the political perspective, the core aim of VAAs is to facilitate decision-making processes and enhance citizen's participation in e-Democracy. However, the impact of the VAAs on the voters' turnout vote is still subject of discussions. Some researchers claim the positive effect (Garzia & Marschall, 2012), others neutral (Fivaz & Schwarz, 2007), while some of them are more sceptical (Walgrave et al., 2009). As already mentioned, VAAs' matching between voter and candidates is entirely based on a number of defined political statements, which has multiple issues. A profile similarity alone may not be enough to guarantee high-quality recommendations. A number of statements that are used to create political profiles are limited and relevant only to the elections in question. Walgrave et al. (2009) show that depending on the statement configuration, VAAs can favour certain parties/candidates in contrast to others and very limited in terms of taking advantage of the voter community in order to enable advanced features like collaborative vote suggestions or interactions between voters.

A further advancement of VAAs represents a web-based application so-called Participa Inteligente. Participa Inteligente is an academic project that arises from the concern for citizen misinformation about policy statements and allows citizens to generate spaces for discussion and participation in topics of interest to the society (Terán & Mancera, 2017). This platform aims to enhance civic participation and empowerment by providing different types of recommendations (political topics, groups, articles and users, among others) according to the citizens' needs. This project expects to facilitate citizens' decision-making by giving them more information and resources to debate. However, the extent of citizens' willingness to actively participate on the platform will depend on the personal desire of disclosure within a political context. This platform is used as an application case for the development of citizen privacy profile framework of the thesis.

Citizen Privacy Profile Framework

This section presents a citizen privacy profile (CPP) framework which is a part of the general system architecture presented in Fig. 4.1, Sect. 4.1.2. The central part of the framework is a citizen's profiles provided with a privacy management tool to preserve privacy on Participa Inteligente platform. The CPP framework (displayed in Fig. 3.2) reflects an environment where the main actor is a citizen who can set up her profile privacy settings within the platform. The components of the framework are designed according to the needs of the VAAs and are based on the concepts of *MyPolitics* and *OurPolitics* as introduced by Ladner and Meier (2014). *MyPolitics* is a personal political diary, where citizen may store her political preferences, VAAs evaluations and individual opinions about elections, as well as electronic votes. According to the citizen's desire for disclosure, she may partly open her political diary to individuals, family members, friends or various communities.

On the other hand, there exists the *OurPolitics* option: if the citizen wants to focus more on her individual political preferences, she can become a member of the non-profit platform of OurPolitics. Eventually the data shared to OurPolitics

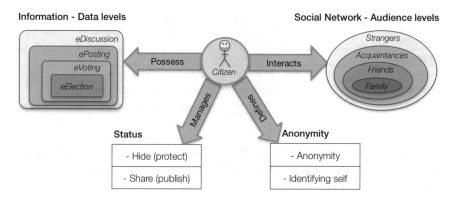

Fig. 3.2 Citizen privacy profile framework (Meier et al., 2018)

could also feed *public memory*. In OurPolitics, the users can meet other citizens or politicians with similar preferences and exchange ideas and information. It is worth noting that the political context of the platform does not affect the basic structure of the privacy management strategies, and therefore, the design of the framework was also influenced by related work in social networking sites (Aïmeur et al., 2009; Fang & LeFevre, 2010; Johnson et al., 2012; Liu & Terzi, 2010; Stutzman et al., 2012). Within the framework, citizens can define privacy settings for their political profiles. The framework consists of five main components: the citizen, the data levels, the audience levels, the status and the anonymity.

The Citizen The central part of the frameworks is the citizen who is using the privacy management tool. The citizen representation includes different demographical variables (culture, age, gender, occupation etc.) and the citizen's role on the platform can be related to the voter, political candidate or political party representative. Moreover, it is the citizen who manages the four components of the framework, including the citizen *possesses* her own data, the citizen *interacts* with her social network, the citizen *manages* the visibility of her data to the particular level of the audience and, finally, the citizen *defines* the anonymity of her shared information.

The Data Levels Citizens' privacy settings reflect their decisions on information disclosure. In his work, Knijnenburg and Kobsa (2013) discovered that user information disclosure is highly dependent on the information context. Indeed, the development of social VAAsVAAs is intended to involve diversified types of political data that contain a rich context. Therefore, four data levels are proposed, as follows: *e-Election, e-Voting, e-Posting and e-Discussion*. These data levels have been inferred from the process steps of e-Voting and e-Election described by Meier (2012). Each data level contains different types of data, as displayed in Table 3.1.

However, the context of different data types could be perceived individually by each person. The framework allows citizens to express their own perceptions on data levels in terms of their degree of importance. A specific colour corresponds to

Table 3.1 Data levels and data types (Kaskina & Meier, 2016)

Data level	Data type
e-Election	Votes for candidates, parties
e-Voting	Votes for political issues, referendums
e-Posting	Participation in blogs, posting on the personal wall
e-Discussion	Discussion topics, questions, answers in discussion forums

the degree of importance which the citizen allots to the data. The most important and valuable data is stored in the core of the component, whereas the less valuable information is set on the outer layers (see Fig. 3.2).

The Audience Levels Following the citizen's perceptions on data types, the citizen's decision depends on the information disclosure to a particular group of people (Knijnenburg & Kobsa, 2013). Therefore, the second component of the framework belongs to the audience levels that will be derived from *the social network* of the citizen. The audience levels are based on social relationships and behavioural mechanisms used to regulate the desired levels of privacy, as presented by Altman (1977). As a result, audience levels have been classified as peripheral relationship bonds represented by strangers and acquaintances, more extensive relationship bonds such as in-laws and friends and close relationship bonds such as family members. Similar to the data levels, each person can perceive her audience levels differently in terms of the relationship bonds. The extent of the relationship bond is also indicated by both colour and layer. The family members are in the core of the component as the closest bonds of the citizen, and strangers and acquaintances are in the outer layers as the peripheral bonds of the citizen.

The Status Finally, the citizen, according to her privacy decision, assigns a particular sharing status: share or hide. Assigning a share status on a particular data type to a particular audience means that this data is open to people for opinion exchange, feedback, discussion or interaction. The hide status means that the citizen wishes to keep her data private and unpublished.

The Anonymity This is an optional functionality for the citizen, where they can define their identity, whether they are sharing the data anonymously or by identifying themself. The non-anonymous nature of the many other online platforms invisibly controls users' self-disclosure so that providing an idealised projection of the real-life "actual self" (Krasnova et al., 2009). Including a function of anonymous disclosure aids users for the desired freedom of self-representation. The user decides on their identity while engaged on the political platform which requires an additional decision-making effort. Therefore, the anonymity functionality is added as an option and is separate from the *status* component of the framework. Depersonalisation or identity of oneself is a very broad privacy-related topic which has many factors to consider. Therefore, it is accounted in the design of the framework but not used during the further research of this thesis.

Table 3.2 Example of a citizen's privacy settings

Data levels	eElection	eVoting	ePosting	eDiscussion
Audience levels				
Strangers	0	0	1	1
Acquaintances	0	0	1	1
Friends	0	1	1	0
Family	0	1	1	0

We assume a set of n citizens $C = \{\vec{c_1}, \vec{c_2}, \ldots, \vec{c_i}, \ldots, \vec{c_N}\}$. According to the CPP framework, we define a set of $k = 4$ audience levels given by the set of {*"Strangers"*, *"Acquaintances"*, *"Friends"*, *"Family"*} and a set of $j = 4$ data levels given by the following set {*"eElection"*, *"eVoting"*, *"ePosting"*, *"eDiscussion"*}. Each citizen $\vec{c_i}$ has to define a set of privacy settings $S = \{s_{11}, s_{11}, \ldots, s_{kj}, \ldots, s_{44}\}$. Thus, the privacy setting is represented as a couple of {*k-th audience level; j-th data level*}. According to the CPP framework, a given citizen $\vec{c_i}$ has two possible statuses: *share* or *hide*. Then, each privacy setting s_{kj} can take values of 1 if citizen $\vec{c_i}$ has shared the data level j to the audience level k, and 0 otherwise. The formalisation of the anonymity of the sharing status is omitted as it is not involved in the research of this thesis.

Table 3.2 displays an example of the privacy settings configuration. A particular citizen considers e-Election data very important to be shared with someone, and therefore, they keep this data private (hide status). However, they decide to share e-Voting data with their family and friends, while they would like to share e-Posting data across all their social networks. Yet, they prefer their e-Discussion-related data is kept visible only to acquaintances and strangers.

There are two privacy settings' properties: *data sensitivity* and *data visibility*. *The sensitivity* is defined by the citizen's decision to share a particular data level represented as a couple of {*data level, status*}. *The visibility* captures the audience level chosen for sharing a particular data level identified as {*audience level, status*}. The example above shows that e-Election data can be perceived to be very sensitive, whereas e-Posting data is less sensitive to get the share status. Also, the visibility of e-Posting is higher than e-Voting, whereas e-Voting and e-Discussion have similar sensitivity but different visibility values.

3.1.3 Evaluation of CPP Framework

To evaluate the proposed framework and study users' privacy attitudes towards using VAAs, we conducted an online survey (Kaskina & Meier, 2016). The survey consisted of four multiple-choice questions, with four possible answers, where questions were designed according to the sharing matrix as shown in Table 3.2. Respondents were explicitly asked to express their preferences on the profile privacy settings as if they had been using the VAAs platform. The questions in the survey were constructed according to the privacy framework components (excluding the anonymity component). Respectively, each question was seeking to determine a person's willingness to share a particular data level. Each multiple-choice answer had a checkbox related to the group of people (audience level) with whom the respondent wished to share the data. If the person left an empty checkbox, it was considered that the data level was kept private (hidden). In total, 70 people were asked to express their privacy preferences; 57% were representatives of Central Asia and 43% were representatives of European countries. The respondents' ages ranged from 22 to 35 years. As a result, a 70-by-16 matrix dataset was collected. Each row of the matrix represents a person, and each column represents a person's assigned values to privacy settings. To measure the sensitivity and visibility of the data within the proposed framework, we calculated the total number of "*share*" occurrences in each privacy setting's attributes {*data level, audience level*}. The results are displayed in Fig. 3.3 and Table 3.3.

First, according to Table 3.3, people clearly tend to consider, within the VAAs, e-Voting and e-Election as the most sensitive data, whereas e-Posting and e-Discussion are perceived as the least sensitive data. Second, it can be concluded that people consider friends and family as the most reliable and trustworthy audience with whom they wish to share their political data, and, thus, most of the data

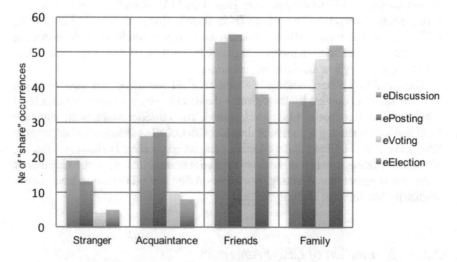

Fig. 3.3 Privacy settings distribution (Kaskina & Meier, 2016)

Table 3.3 Data sensitivity and visibility (Kaskina & Meier, 2016)

Sensitivity		Visibility	
Data level	% of "share"	Audience level	% of "share"
e-Discussion	47.8%	Friends	67.5%
e-Posting	46.7%	Family	61.4%
e-Voting	37.5%	Acquaintances	25.3%
e-Election	36.7%	Strangers	14.6%

is visible to friends and family. However, from the privacy settings distribution, a dependency can be noticed between users' perceptions of the data sensitivity and visibility. For example, Fig. 3.3 illustrates that, for some, the sensitivity of the data increases from e-Discussion to e-Election when it is visible to strangers, acquaintances and friends, while it decreases from e-Discussion to e-Election when it is visible to family. Moreover, the sensitivity of e-Election and e-Voting is lowest when visible to family and friends, whereas the highest sensitivity is observed when visible to strangers and acquaintances. The extent of visibility (a chosen audience for sharing the data) directly depends on the data sensitivity. However, privacy preferences might vary considerably between different people; therefore, a clustering technique was applied to group people based on their privacy preferences.

The goal of applying a clustering technique to the dataset is to classify groups of people based on their privacy preferences. Clustering is an unsupervised learning task, where a clustering algorithm organises a given set of objects into similar groups (clusters). Objects belonging to the same cluster are as similar as possible to each other. Citizens will be similar with their feature vector expressing their privacy preferences, and, as a result, the groups of like-minded participants are identified. Since the collected dataset of survey participants represented a binary data, the *k-modes* clustering algorithm is applied. The k-modes is an extension of the k-means to deal with categorical binary data. In the k-modes, we use new dissimilarity measures to deal with categorical objects, replace means of clusters with modes and use a frequency-based method to update modes in the clustering process to minimise the clustering cost function (Huang, 1997). According to the number of audience levels, the initial number of clusters was set to four. Using a built-in function of the R package $klaR$,[1] after 4 iterations, the clustering produced four groups of participants (Fig. 3.4).

Partitioning people into clusters allowed us to distinguish patterns of disclosure preferences of the particular data types to the audience levels. In Fig. 3.4, each table represented characteristics of each of four clusters. The coloured cells in the tables display the vector values of the cluster prototypes produced by k-modes clustering. The percentage numbers indicate a number of "share" statuses on each privacy setting attribute {*data level, audience level*} within a cluster. After inspecting Fig. 3.4, the following four classifications of participants can be identified: *Cluster 1*—people are willing to share all data levels with friends; *Cluster 2*—people are willing to share all data levels with family and friends, where they also tend to share e-Posting and e-Discussion to acquaintances; *Cluster 3*—people tend to share all data levels only with their family; *Cluster 4*—the smallest number of people who are willing to share all data to friends and family only. In Cluster 3, it can be observed that while people are only family-oriented data sharers, there are some proportion of people who also disclose e-Posting and e-Discussion data to friends. Similar sub-tendencies of sharing e-Posting and e-Discussion data to friends can be found in Cluster 1 and Cluster 4. However, according to the k-modes algorithm, those with

---

[1] https://cran.r-project.org/web/packages/klaR/klaR.pdf.

Clust1 = 25	Stran.	Acq.	Frien.	Fam.
eElection	1.6%	3.2%	12.1%	5.6%
eVoting	1.6%	4%	16.9%	4%
ePosting	2.4%	6.5%	14%	2.4%
eDiscussion	4.8%	4.8%	13.7%	1.6%

Clust2 = 20	Stran.	Acq.	Frien.	Fam.
eElection	0.9%	1.9%	8%	9.4%
eVoting	0.5%	2.3%	8%	8.9%
ePosting	3.3%	8%	9.4%	8.9%
eDiscussion	3.8%	8%	9.4%	9.4%

Clust3 = 20	Stran.	Acq.	Frien.	Fam.
eElection	0%	0%	1.1%	21.5%
eVoting	0%	0%	0%	20.4%
ePosting	2.2%	2.2%	12.9%	10.8%
eDiscussion	4.3%	3.2%	11.8%	9.7%

Clust4 = 5	Stran.	Acq.	Frien.	Fam.
eElection	2.3%	0%	11.6%	11.6%
eVoting	2.3%	0%	11.6%	11.6%
ePosting	2.3%	0%	11.6%	9.3%
eDiscussion	2.3%	0%	11.6%	11.6%

Fig. 3.4 Cluster characteristics

similar sharing sub-tendencies were sharply assigned to different clusters. This is a disadvantage of sharp clustering when compared with fuzzy clustering techniques. In the later sections, the advantages of fuzzy clustering techniques will be discussed (Sect. 3.3.1).

3.2   Implementation of CPP

3.2.1   Platform Description

This section introduces the actual implementation of the citizen privacy profile(CPP) framework for the specified case of voting advice applications (VAAs). The *Participa Inteligente* (PI) web-based platform[2] is an academic project developed and endorsed by the University of Fribourg. The main functionality of the platform is to serve as a voting advice application, where citizens, according to their political preferences, are provided with recommendations. PI generates an online space for discussions and citizens' participation on topics of political interest. PI was launched in December 2016 within the campaign for the 2017 Ecuador national elections which took place in April 2017. The platform was developed in the Drupal[3] environment. The system consists of different platform blocks, type of content and user roles which will be discussed in the following subsections. The main focus of

---

[2] https://participacioninteligente.org/.
[3] https://www.drupal.org/.

this section is the integration of the CPP framework into PI and the implementation of privacy settings for the users' profiles.

Platform Blocks

The three main platform's blocks are the timeline, the voting advice application and user profiles. The timeline block displays twitter feeds from presidential candidates, vice president and the political assembly. The voting advice application block represents a questionnaire based on political policy topics and further based on users' and candidates' profile to calculate recommendations for the closest presidential/assembly candidates to the particular user. The user profiles block differentiates between candidates/assembly and user (citizen) profiles. Candidate profiles are created by experts, answers provided by candidates themselves and derived from the twitter accounts of candidates. Users' profiles are created by citizens.

Type of Content

A different type of data content can be generated in the platform. *Social Network* represents users' social connections, such as unidirectional "follow" relations or bidirectional "friend" relations. *Static data* is the users' input which does not change its initial value over the time, like personal information (name, date of birth, gender, province of voting, vote intention etc.), user's question to the forum. *Dynamic data* relates to the activity in the platform (the collective number of points gained for offensive content/comments, invitations, published articles, reads etc.), explicit ratings on political topic interest (economy—9 stars, well-being—5 stars etc.), articles (user creates post of the text, video or image placed on their wall), answers to voting advice application questionnaire or attitudes on published data (comments, reactions, vote up/down, negative/positive).

User Roles

There are three user roles in the platform: administration, political candidate and user (citizen). The administration role has all permissions for administering the platform and represented by the university developers. The political candidate role has similar permissions as the citizen role, besides that political candidate is obliged to provide answers to the policy questions which are further filled by experts. A user role is assigned to every registered citizen in the platform.

3.2.2 Privacy Settings Functionality

It can be observed that a significant amount of diverse personal data can be generated by users while participating on the platform. Being able to manage privacy of one's profile is a necessary functionality both for this platform and for this research. To develop a privacy management tool where users will be able to define privacy settings for their profiles, the CPP framework proposed in Sect. 3.1.2 is adapted for the PI platform (see Fig. 3.5). Similarly, to the CPP framework, in the PI platform, the user decides which data can be seen by other users in the platform. By sharing particular data, a user defines to which audience the intended data is visible or not. The audience is derived from the user's social network. However, while adapting to the case of the PI platform, there have been several applied alterations to the original CPP framework, as discussed below.

Information: Data Levels

Compared to the original CPP, the colour and the layer position of the data level in the PI platform do not indicate the increasing, or decreasing, degree of data importance. Instead, the data layers have dashed lines which explicate that the importance of a particular data may vary depending on each person. The data levels and related data types in the CPP of the PI are described in Table 3.4. There is a new added setting named "contactability", which permits other users of the platform to contact a particular user. Thus, the user can decide which person from their social network can contact them via private message.

Figure 3.6 shows the implementation of the privacy settings for the five data levels—PersonalInformation, VoteIntention, MyActivity, MyTopics and MyRelations. By clicking on the checkbox, the user shares a particular data level to the public space of the platform. If the checkbox is left unticked, then the data level stays private and only visible to the owner of the user profile. It is important to note that

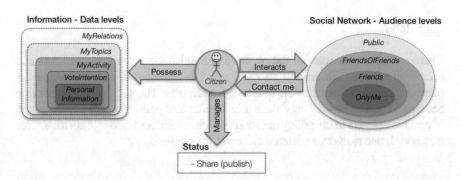

Fig. 3.5 CPP framework for the Participa Inteligente platform

Table 3.4 Data levels and data types

Data level	Data type
Personal information	Name, date of birth, gender, province of vote, level of education, level of interest in politics
VoteIntention	Users' answer about the intended candidate to vote for
MyActivity	Users' activity on the platform—collective number of points gained for the provided answers and comments in the forum, number of articles read, number of posted articles, marked supplied offensive content, invitations
MyTopics	Explicit ratings of interest in political topics—economy, education, international politics, public politics, security, society
MyRelations	The list of users' friends and followers
Contact Me	The contactability of profile—who can contact the user on the platform via private message

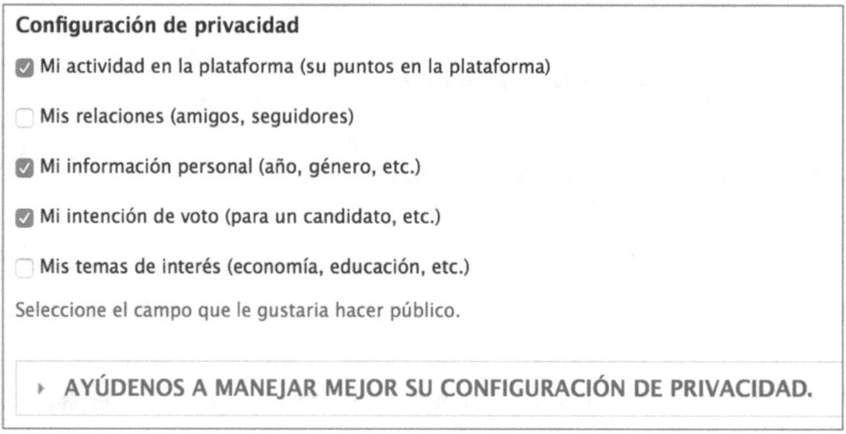

Configuración de privacidad

☑ Mi actividad en la plataforma (su puntos en la plataforma)

☐ Mis relaciones (amigos, seguidores)

☑ Mi información personal (año, género, etc.)

☑ Mi intención de voto (para un candidato, etc.)

☐ Mis temas de interés (economía, educación, etc.)

Seleccione el campo que le gustaria hacer público.

▸ AYÚDENOS A MANEJAR MEJOR SU CONFIGURACIÓN DE PRIVACIDAD.

Fig. 3.6 Privacy settings

by selecting the data level for disclosure, all related data types within this data level will be visible. In other words, the privacy setting is applied to the whole set of the data level and not for a particular data type. In the PI platform, the CPP framework has only one status for the disclosure—"share (publish)" (see Fig. 3.5). It does not contain a "hide" status as CPP has an altered social network structure which does not require applying the status "hide". Particularly, the "hide" was substituted with the "ShareToMe" status. As the anonymity is not considered in this research, the anonymity component was also eliminated from the framework. Thus, the function in Fig. 3.6 implements an actual privacy setting, whereas the module of audience selection depicted in Fig. 3.7 requests users to express their opinions to specific parts of their social network (audience levels) where a particular data level can be visible. This module does not affect the actual configuration of the profile visibility, and it solely collects users' sharing opinions of the data levels among their audience

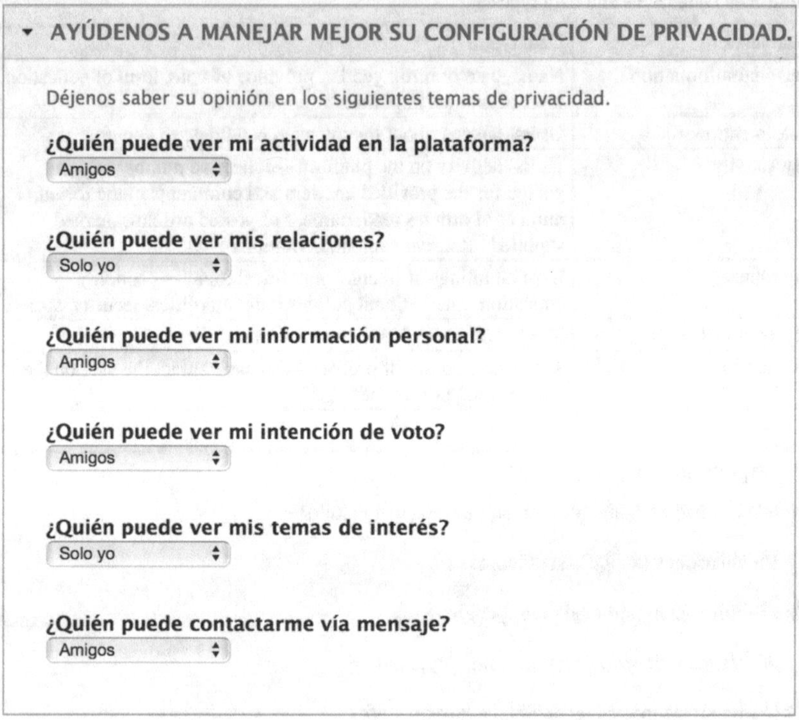

Fig. 3.7 Audience selection

levels. The actual effect of privacy settings is performed by the module displayed in Fig. 3.6.

Social Network: Audience Levels

Conversely from the CPP framework (Sect. 3.1.2), the social network structure has the following audience levels: *1—only me*, i.e., sharing to the family in real-case applications is not a common functionality, for the PI the audience level of the "family" was substituted with "only me"; *2—friends*, *3—friends of friends* and *4—* visible to *public* space (Fig. 3.5). An indispensable part of the user's privacy decision relies on the audience, whether the data is visible to particular audience or not. To build up a social network, two types of relations are defined within PI platform: friend and follower relations (Figs. 3.8 and 3.9). Having friends relations, the graph of the user's social network can be built and the friends of friends relations can be calculated.

Fig. 3.8 Add a friend/follower

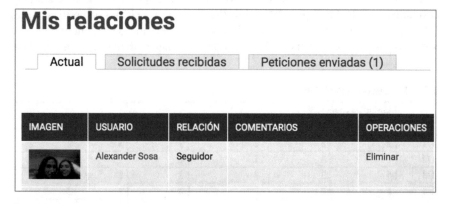

Fig. 3.9 A list of user's relations

3.2.3 Privacy Profiles Extraction

Unlike the preliminary research presented in Sect. 3.1.2, where data was collected from a survey, this dataset consists of expressed user privacy preferences towards sharing their political data levels to a particular part of their social network while engaged in the registration process on the PI platform. The dataset was collected during the 3-month period of December 2016–February 2017. In this study we investigated information disclosure behaviour of users, precisely, to which audience they prefer to share the data levels of the profile. In the platform, the users' privacy settings are stored in a MySQL database.

It is worth noting that for users who did not set up their preferences in Fig. 3.7, the default privacy settings were set up to public visibility. For our investigation, we had extracted users' privacy settings from the MySQL database on which the PI operates. The dataset represents a set of user vectors with six dimensions related to the data levels—{MyActivity, ContactMe, MyRelations, MyTopics, PersonalInformation and VoteIntention}. Each data level can take four values by assigning a sharing status to a particular audience level in sets {1 means "OnlyMe", 2 - Friends, 3 - FriendsOfFriends, 4 - Public} as seen in Table 3.5. Following dataset cleaning and analysis preparation, the final data consisted of 391 user privacy profiles. This consisted of 131 females, 253 males and 7 users who did not provide gender information. The age of users is between 23 and 36 (median age is 28).

The explorative analysis unveils preliminary tendencies in the dataset. According to Table 3.5, there are six variables (dimensions) in the dataset. The correlations analysis displayed in Table 3.6 enables an investigation into whether those variables are independent or if they are interdependent and correlated.

Table 3.6 indicates that the highest correlation is between the MyActivity and MyRelations data, indicating that they are dependent and have similar sharing tendencies. It is also interesting to note that the MyActivity data is strongly correlated with the MyTopics data, while the disclosure decisions on political topics (MyTopics) are in turn correlated with disclosure decision on VoteIntention. The visibility preferences of PersonalInfo strongly correlate with the MyRelations data.

Table 3.5 Dataset description

User	Variables (data types)					
	MyActivity	ContactMe	MyRelations	MyTopics	PersInf	VoteIntention
U1	2	3	2	3	3	2
U2	1	3	1	1	1	1
U3	4	3	3	2	1	1
U4	1	2	2	2	2	2
...	...	...	...	...	...	...
U391	4	4	4	2	2	1

Table 3.6 Data levels correlations

	MyActivity	ContactMe	MyRelations	MyTopics	PersonalInfo
MyActivity					
ContactMe	0.40****				
MyRelations	0.72****	0.39****			
MyTopics	0.64****	0.43****	0.56****		
PersonalInfo	0.56****	0.34****	0.64****	0.52****	
VoteIntention	0.58****	0.34****	0.58****	0.60****	0.59****

(1) **** $p < .0001$; *** $p < .001$; ** $p < .01$; * $p < .05$

Noticeably, a higher variance is observed with the ContactMe dimension. This can be justified with the fact that this variable does not perceptually relate as a data level as it was designed as the functionality to allow other users to contact oneself. In contrast, other variables directly represent the disclosure of the data, and therefore the ContactMe variable scored the lowest correlations among those variables.

In general, the dataset showed that there were only positive correlations. There exist tendencies in disclosing political information, such as if the MyActivity data is open to the public, then MyRelation is also open to the public. However, correlation among variables indicates dependencies among them, as well as the lack of independent variables. Potentially the political context of the platform affects different data types that are well correlated, such as the disclosure behaviour of VoteIntention depends on what decisions were taken when disclosing political topics of the user. However, the correlation analysis is not sufficient to make final conclusions on the dataset. For example, there are correlations with low p-values, between ContactMe and VoteIntention and between PersonalInformation and MyTopics. Thus, there is a chance of existence of multidimensional privacy profiles which the following section discusses in detail.

3.3   User Privacy Profiles Modelling

This thesis applies different fuzzy clustering algorithms on the dataset of users' privacy profiles. This section illustrates how a user with the multidimensional privacy profile can belong to several clusters to some certain degree of belonging. Knowing this additional information can reduce an oversimplification problem on estimating user's privacy behaviour and improve the model accuracy. We explore different fuzzy clustering algorithms parametrized with different distance metrics.

3.3.1   Fuzzy Clustering

Dataset Clustering Tendency

As clustering is an unsupervised machine learning, and in our case the existing number of clusters is unknown, we will analyse the dataset's tendency to be clustered into groups. Also, analysing the feasibility of the clustering analysis helps avoid meaningless clustering. The method of a visual assessment of cluster tendency (VAT) was applied using the R package "fclust"[4] originally described by Bezdek and Hathaway (2002). This approach can be used to visually inspect the clustering tendency of the dataset. It computes the dissimilarity matrix between the objects in

---

[4] https://cran.r-project.org/web/packages/fclust/fclust.pdf.

Fig. 3.10 Visual assessment
of cluster tendency

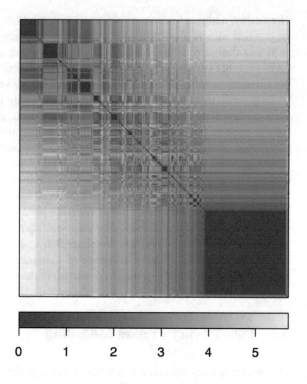

the dataset using a Euclidean distance measure and then reorders the dissimilarity matrix so that similar objects are close to one another. Darkly shaded diagonal blocks correspond to assumed clusters in the data. Therefore, k dark blocks along the main diagonal suggest that the data contain k assumed clusters. The size of each block represents the approximate size of the cluster (Giordani & Ferraro, 2015). The visual clustering assessment indicated the existence of four explicitly dark blocks (clusters), where there is a block in the left-side top that appears to contain several sub-blocks. From this figure, a potential fuzziness of user privacy profile can already be observed, which is represented by possible existence of those small subclusters (Fig. 3.10).

This thesis focuses on the application of fuzzy clustering techniques as they better deal with overlapped cluster structures. To demonstrate the advantage of fuzzy clustering, Fig. 3.11 displays the plot with classic k-means clustering (R function *kmeans()*), whereas Fig. 3.12 plots the partition produced by the fuzzy c-means clustering algorithm (R package "e1071" function *cmeans()*). Both use the Euclidean distance with four clusters. When considering the selected regions of data points on both plots, it can be seen that sharp k-means clustering hardly distinguishes the overlapped cluster 2 and cluster 3 and produces a mixed distribution of its points, whereas fuzzy clustering could perform a better identification of the overlapped clusters structure. Now, unlike to the k-means results, users 375, 69, 234 and 215 belong to the same cluster. Also, all four clusters are better separated

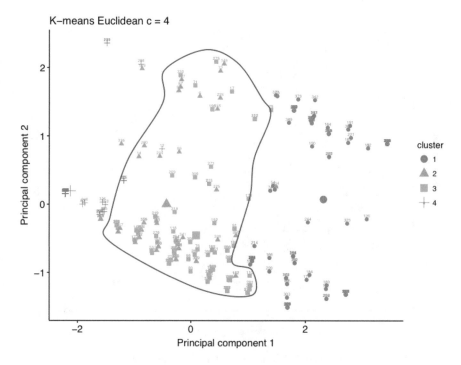

Fig. 3.11 K-means clustering with Euclidean norm of four cluster partitions

when compared to the k-means cluster separation. In this research, fuzzy clustering algorithms are chosen against sharp clustering.

Table 3.7 outlines the characteristics of the fuzzy clustering algorithms used for this research, particularly, what type of cluster, shape the algorithm is capable to detect, including the required input parameters to run the clustering technique. The detailed algorithms of both techniques are described in the subsequent sections.

Fuzzy C-Means Clustering

The main objective of the Fuzzy C-means (FCM) algorithm is to compute the similarity between an object shared with each cluster using a membership function. The membership function calculates the membership degree of each object in every cluster with values in the range of [0,1]. A high degree of similarity between the object and a cluster is assigned when a membership value is close to 1, whereas values close to 0 imply a low similarity between the object and that cluster (Bezdek et al., 1984). Initially proposed by Dunn (1973), this algorithm was later improved by Bezdek who introduced the idea of a fuzzification parameter m in the range $[1, N]$, which determines the degree of fuzziness in clusters. When $m = 1$, the effect is a crisp clustering of points, when $m > 1$ the degree of fuzziness among points increases.

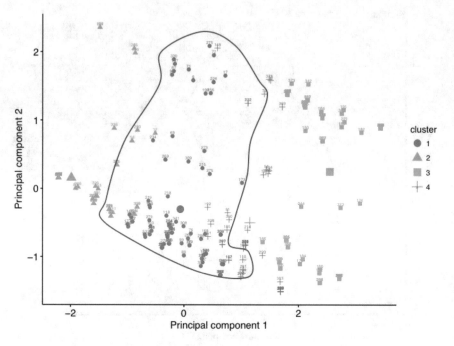

Fig. 3.12 FCM clustering with Euclidean norm of four cluster partitions

Table 3.7 Overview of the used fuzzy clustering algorithms

	Algorithm structure								
	Clusters		Shape		Input parameters				
	Crisp	Fuzzy	Sphere	Ellipse	m fuzzifier	Stop criteria	Iter.	Dist.	n of clust.
FCM		x	x		x	x	x	x	x
PAM	x	x	x	x		x		x	x

With FCM clustering, it is possible to obtain hard c-partitions, while with hard clustering it is impossible to determine fuzzy c-partitions. Therefore, the advantage of FCM clustering is that an observation can belong entirely to one cluster and, at the same time, have a partial membership in several fuzzy clusters. In addition, FCM clustering helps in dealing with undistinctive data. FCM attempts to find the most characteristic point in each cluster, which can be considered as the "centroid" of the cluster and, then, the membership degree for each object in the clusters. This goal is achieved by minimising *the objective function*, which is defined as follows (Wang & Zhang, 2007):

$$Minimise\, J_m(U, V) = \sum_{i=1}^{N}\sum_{j=1}^{C} u_{ij}^{m}||x_i - c_j||^2 \tag{3.1}$$

where N is the number of data points in a given dataset, C is the number of clusters required, $X = \{x_1, x_2, \ldots, x_N\} \subset R^S$ is the feature data, $V = \{c_1, c_2, \ldots, c_C\} \subset R^S$ are cluster centroids, and $U = [u_{ij}]_{C \times N}$ is a fuzzy partition matrix composed of the membership degrees of the i-th data point x_i in cluster j. The norm, $\|x_i - c_j\|$, measures the similarity (or closeness) of the data point x_i to the centre vector c_j of cluster j. According to Bezdek et al. (1984), different norms can be used, such as Euclidean, diagonal or Mahalanobis. In each iteration, the algorithm maintains a centre vector for each of the clusters. These cluster centres are calculated as the weighted average of the population, where the weights are given by the degrees of membership stored in the membership matrix. *The cluster centre* vector c_j is calculated according to the formula, Eq. (3.2):

$$c_j = \frac{\sum_{i=1}^{N} u_{ij}^m \cdot x_i}{\sum_{i=1}^{N} u_{ij}^m} \tag{3.2}$$

where u_{ij} is the value of the degree of membership calculated in the previous iteration. *The membership matrix* contains the membership degree of each observation to a cluster and is calculated according to the formula, Eq. (3.3):

$$u_{ij} = \frac{1}{\sum_{k=1}^{C} \left(\frac{\|x_i - c_j\|}{\|x_i - c_k\|} \right)^{\frac{2}{m-1}}} \tag{3.3}$$

where $\|x_i - c_j\|$ is the distance from the observation i to current cluster centre j, $\|x_i - c_k\|$ is the distance from the observation i to other cluster centre k and m is—the fuzziness coefficient.

At the start of the algorithm, the degree of membership of the observation to cluster k is initialised with a random value. In Eq. (3.1) and Eq. (3.3), the fuzziness coefficient m, where $1 < m < \infty$, measures the tolerance of the required clustering. This value determines how much the clusters can overlap with one another. The higher the value of m, the larger the overlap between clusters. The required accuracy of the degree of membership determines the number of iterations completed by the FCM algorithm. This measure of accuracy is calculated using the degree of membership from one iteration to the next, taking the largest of these values across all data points while considering all of the clusters. If we represent the measure of accuracy between iteration k and $k + 1$, then iterations will stop at *the convergence condition $max_{ij} \{|u_{ij}^{(k+1)} - u_{ij}^{(k)}|\} < \epsilon$*, where ϵ is a termination criterion between 0 and 1, whereas k is the iteration steps. This procedure converges to a local minimum.

The FCM algorithm is a perfect solution when the initial number of clusters is known, if not, then determining the optimal number of cluster for a dataset is an important requirement. Defining an optimal number of clusters is referred to the term of a cluster validity and will be discussed in Sect. 3.3.2. The calculation of FCM algorithm is performed with R package "e1071",[5] function *cmeans()*. The function *cmeans()* randomly selects cluster centroid values with the weighting exponent m=2 used as the best recommended value for calculations of fuzzy clustering (Pal & Bezdek, 1995).

Partitioning Around Medoids Clustering

When partitioning a set of objects into k clusters, the initial objective is to find clusters in each with the objects represented by a high degree of similarity, while objects belonging to different clusters are as dissimilar as possible. The algorithm of the Partitioning Around Medoids (PAM), proposed by Kaufman and Rousseeuw (2009), searches for the k representative objects, named *medoids* among objects in the given dataset. In contrast to traditional FCM algorithm, where centroids are calculated as artificial object means, these medoids are computed such that the total dissimilarity of all objects to their nearest medoid is minimal.

The algorithm of PAM consists of two phases: *build* and *swap*. In the *build* phase, an initial clustering is obtained by the successive selection of representative objects until k objects have been found. The first object is the one for which the sum of the dissimilarities to all other objects is as small as possible. This object is the most centrally located within the set of objects. Subsequently, at each step, another object is selected. This object is the one which decreases the objective function as much as possible. To find this object, the following steps are carried out:

1. Consider the object i which has not yet been selected.
2. Consider a non-selected object j and calculate the difference between its dissimilarity D_j with the most similar previously selected object and its dissimilarity $d(j, i)$ with object i.
3. If this difference is positive, object j will contribute to the decision to select object i. Therefore, the following is calculated:

$$C_{ji} = max(D_j - d(j, i), 0) \tag{3.4}$$

4. Calculate the total gain obtained by selecting object i:

$$\sum_j C_{ji} \tag{3.5}$$

5. Choose the not yet selected object i which

$$maximises_i \sum_j C_{ji} \tag{3.6}$$

---

[5] https://cran.r-project.org/web/packages/e1071/index.html.

This process is continued until k objects have been found. The second phase *swap* of the PAM algorithm attempts to improve the set of representative objects and the clustering derived by this set. This is achieved by considering all pairs of objects (i, h) for which *object i has been selected and object h is not*. It is determined what effect is obtained on the values of the clustering when a swap is carried out, as when object i is no longer selected as a representative object but object h is.

To calculate the effect of a swap between i and h on the clustering, the following calculations are carried out:

1. Consider a non-selected object j and calculate its contribution C_{jih} to the swap:

   (a) If j is further from both i and h than from one of the other representative objects, C_{jih} is zero.
   (b) If j is not further from i than from any other selected representative object $(d(j, i) = D_j)$, two situations must be considered: *(i)* j is closer to h than to the second closest representative object $d(j, h) < E_j$, where E_j is the dissimilarity between j and the second most similar representative object. In this case the contribution of object j to the swap between objects i and h is $C_{jih} = d(j, h) - d(j, i)$, and *(ii)* j is at least as distant from h from the second closest representative object $d(j, h) \geq E_j$. In this case the contribution of object j to the swap is $C_{jih} = E_j - D_j$. It should be observed that in the situation *(i)* the contribution C_{jih} can either be positive or negative depending on the relative position of objects j, h and i. Only if object j is closer to i than to h is the contribution positive, which indicates that the swap is not favourable from the point of view of object j. On the other hand, in situation *(ii)*, the contribution is always positive because it cannot be advantageous to replace i by an object h further away from j than from the second closest representative object.
   (c) j is more distant from object i than from at least one of the other representative objects, but closer to h than to any representative object. In this case, the contribution of j to the swap is $C_{jih} = d(j, h) - D_j$.

2. Calculate the total result of a swap by adding the contributions C_{jih}: $T_{ih} = \sum_j C_{jih}$. In the next steps it is decided whether or not to carry out a swap.
3. Select the pair (i, h) which *minimises* T_{ih}. If the minimum T_{ih} is negative, the swap is carried out and the algorithm returns to step 1. If the minimum T_{ih} is positive or 0, the value of the objective cannot be decreased by carrying out a swap and, as such, the algorithm stops.

The objective function of PAM algorithm solely depends on the dissimilarity between objects, and therefore, the algorithm can be parametrised with different distance metrics. The fuzzy membership degrees for each object are calculated as a probability (in a range [0,1]) of the belonging based on the distance between observations and medoids. The benefit of this algorithm is that it looks through a real-case privacy profiles and chooses the cluster centres (medoids) from a true existing privacy profile of the population. Moreover, it does not require initial guesses for the cluster centroids, unlike in FCM algorithm. This point is advantageous, especially for the case of this research, when there is no prior knowledge about cluster centres in the dataset. PAM algorithm is more robust than FCM in the presence of noise and outliers as a medoid is less influenced by outliers or other extreme values than a mean. However, the processing is not as cost effective (Rokach & Maimon, 2005). The calculation of PAM algorithm is performed with *R* package "ClusterR",[6] function *cluster_medoids()*.

Measuring Distances

An important issue in clustering is to decide how the similarity between data points should be defined in order to form clusters where the data points have a high similarity to each other and a low similarity to data points from other clusters. The proximity between two data points identifies its closeness which can be expressed in terms of similarity, dissimilarity or distance between two data points. Thus, two data points are close when their dissimilarity or distance is small or their similarity is large. The formal dissimilarity on the set *S* can be defined as a function *d* from $S \times S$ to the real numbers as follows (Portmann, 2012): *(i)* $d(x, y) \geq 0$ for all x, y belonging to *S*, *(ii)* $d(x, y) = 0$ if, and only if, $x = y$, and *(iii)* $d(x, y) = d(x, y)$ for all x, y belonging to *S*. Both aforementioned clustering methods use the distance metric to calculate the similarity between objects. For the clustering implementation, two common distances are used: Euclidean and Manhattan. Also, PAM clustering with Mahalanobis distance is calculated as this distance is entirely different from others and deals with the covariance matrix (Table 3.8). Euclidean distance takes the square root of the sum of the squares of the differences between two points, while Manhattan distance computes the distance that would be travelled to get from one data point to the other if a grid-like path is followed. The Manhattan distance between two items is the sum of the differences of their corresponding

Table 3.8 Overview of distance metrics

Name	Formula		FCM	PAM
Euclidean	$$d = \sqrt{\sum_{i=1}^{n}(x_i - y_i)^2} \qquad (3.7)$$		x	x
Manhattan	$$d = \sum_{i=1}^{n} |x_i - y_i| \qquad (3.8)$$		x	x
Mahalanobis	$$d(\vec{x}, \vec{y}) = \sqrt{(\vec{x} - \vec{y})^T S^{-1}(\vec{x} - \vec{y})} \qquad (3.9)$$			x

---

[6] https://cran.r-project.org/web/packages/ClusterR/ClusterR.pdf.

components. The Mahalanobis distance accounts for the fact that the variances in each direction are different and considers the covariance between variables. It reduces to the familiar Euclidean distance for uncorrelated variables with unit variance.

3.3.2 Evaluation of Clustering Validity

Clustering of the dataset is an unsupervised technique and when the initial number of clusters in the dataset is unknown, then the critical question becomes in defining the right number of potential partitions in the dataset. The issue when finding an optimal c is usually called cluster validity (Wang & Zhang, 2007). To validate whether the clustering technique performed an accurate partitioning of the dataset, the validity function can evaluate the clustering result. In the literature many validity indexes have been proposed for the validation of the dataset partition produced by fuzzy clustering algorithms. Validity indexes are considered to be independent of clustering algorithms (Wu & Yang, 2005).

Most validity indexes search through all c clusters to measure the degree of compactness and separation of an optimal c, so that each of these optimal c clusters is compact and separated from other clusters (Wu & Yang, 2005). *The compactness* measures the closeness of cluster elements, i.e., their variance, where the low variance is an indicator of closeness. *The separation* indicates how distinct two clusters are and computes the "distance" between two different clusters. Thus, the aim of validation indexes has been to locate the clustering that minimises the compactness and maximises the separation (Kim et al., 2004). Table 3.9 outlines the validity indexes used in this research. As shown, the validity indexes differ on the parameters used for the calculation and on its inherent properties of detecting the compactness and separation of data partitions, as well as the criteria for choosing the optimal number of clusters (Table 3.9).

Table 3.9 Overview of validation indexes

| Name | Criteria | Parameters used | | | Property | |
		$U = [u_{ij}]$ [1]	V^2	X^3	Compact	Separation
Partition coefficient	max(PC)	x			x	
Partition entropy	min(PE)	x			x	
Modified partition coefficient	max(MPC)	x			x	
Xie and Beni	min(XBI)	x	x	x	x	x
Crisp Silhouette	max(CS)		x	x		x
Fuzzy Silhouette	max(FS)	x	x	x	x	x

[1] Fuzzy partition matrix (membership degrees)
[2] Set of cluster centroids derived from the clustering result
[3] Initial dataset

Partition Coefficient (PC)

In his work, Bezdek (1974) defined a performance measure based on minimising the overall content of a pairwise fuzzy intersection in U, the partition matrix and, thus, proposed the partition coefficient. The PC index indicates the average relative amount of membership sharing between pairs of fuzzy subsets in U, by combining them into a single number and averaging the contents of pairs of fuzzy algebraic products Wang and Zhang (2007). The PC index was defined as

$$V_{PC} = \frac{1}{n} \sum_{i=1}^{c} \sum_{j=1}^{n} u_{ij}^2 \qquad (3.10)$$

where $\frac{1}{c} \leqslant V_{PC} \leqslant 1$. The optimal cluster number c^* is found through solving $max_{2 \leqslant c \leqslant n-1} V_{PC}$ to produce the best clustering performance for the dataset X.

Partition Entropy (PE)

Another measure of cluster validity using membership matrix as introduced by Bezdek (1974) is a partition entropy. The PE index is a scalar measure of the amount of fuzziness in a given U, Wang and Zhang (2007) defined as

$$V_{PE} = \frac{1}{n} \sum_{i=1}^{c} \sum_{j=1}^{n} u_{ij}^2 log_a u_{ij}^2 \qquad (3.11)$$

where a is the base of the logarithm, $0 \leqslant V_{PE} \leqslant log_a c$. The optimal cluster number c^* is found by solving $min_{2 \leqslant c \leqslant n-1} V_{PE}$ to produce the best clustering performance for the dataset X.

Modified Partition Coefficient (MPC)

To reduce the monotonic evolution tendency with c of PC and PE indexes, Dave (1996) proposed the modification of the V_{PC} index. The modified partition coefficient is defined as

$$V_{MPC} = 1 - -\frac{c}{c-1}(1 - V_{PC}) \qquad (3.12)$$

where $0 \leqslant V_{MPC} \leqslant 1$. The optimal cluster number c^* is found by solving $max_{2 \leqslant c \leqslant n-1} V_{MPC}$ to produce the best clustering performance for the dataset X.

Jiu-Lun Fan and Ma (2000) show that MPC performance to be simpler and more effective. Yet, PC, MPC and PE have received criticism as they use only fuzzy membership values and do not consider geometrical and topological properties of the dataset. Wang and Zhang (2007) enumerate the following drawbacks of these: the monotonous dependency on the number of clusters, the sensitivity to the fuzzifier m and the lack of direct connection to the geometry of the data, as they do not use the data itself. Bezdek (1974) remarked that if the algorithm is not finding a significant cluster substructure in X, it may be the fault of either the algorithm or the data lacking structure. Consequently, the unique minimum V_{PC} (or maximum V_{PE}) is very helpful in deciding when the structure is not being found. In contrast, the following indexes measure both fuzzy memberships and the data structure.

Xie and Beni Index (XBI)

According to Pal and Bezdek (1995), the proposed validity index by Xie and Beni (1991) is the most reliable and proved to have the best response over a wide range of choices for both the number of clusters and the weighting exponent. Modified by Pal and Bezdek (1995), XBI is identified as

$$V_{XBI} = \frac{J_m(u,c)/n}{Sep(c)} = \frac{\sum_{i=1}^{c} \sum_{j=1}^{n} u_{ij}^m ||x_i - c_j||^2}{n \, min_{i,j} ||c_i - cj||^2} \tag{3.13}$$

The XBI index measures both the compactness and the separation of clusters. The V_{XBI} equation's numerator indicates the compactness of the fuzzy partition, while the denominator indicates the strength of the separation between clusters. A good partition produces a small value for the compactness, and that well-separated c_j will produce a high value for the separation. Thus, an optimal c^* is found by solving $min_{2 \leqslant c \leqslant n-1} V_{XBI}$ to produce the best clustering performance for the dataset X.

Crisp Silhouette (CS)

Another more commonly used measure is the Crisp Silhouette (CS). According to Campello and Hruschka (2006) to define this criterion, first you need to consider a data object $j \in \{1, 2, \ldots, N\}$ belonging to cluster $c \in \{1, \ldots, C\}$. In the context of crisp partitions produced by a prototype-based clustering algorithm (e.g., k-means), this means that the object j is closer to the prototype of cluster c than to any other prototype. Then in the context of fuzzy partitions, on the other hand, this means that the membership of the jth object to the pth fuzzy cluster, u_{cj}, is higher than the membership of this object to any other fuzzy cluster, i.e., $u_{cj} > u_{qj}$ for every $q \in \{1, \ldots, c\}, q \neq c$ (Campello & Hruschka, 2006). The silhouette of object j is defined as

$$s_j = \frac{b_{cj} - a_{cj}}{max\{a_{cj}, b_{cj}\}} \tag{3.14}$$

where a_{cj} is an average distance (based on the same norm adopted in the fuzzy clustering algorithm) of object j to all other objects belonging to cluster p, d_{qj} is the average distance of this object to all objects belonging to another cluster $q, q \neq p$ and b_{cj} is the minimum d_{qj} computed over $q = 1, \ldots, c, q \neq c$, which represents the dissimilarity of object j to its closest neighbouring cluster. The denominator of Eq. (3.14) is used solely as a normalisation term. Thus, the higher value of s_j indicates the good assignment of object j to cluster c. In case c is a cluster constituted uniquely by object j, then the silhouette of this object is defined as $s_j = 0$. To prevent such cases, the Crisp Silhouette was defined as the average of s_j over $j = 1, 2, \ldots, N$, i.e.,

$$V_{CS} = \frac{1}{N} \sum_{j=1}^{N} s_j \tag{3.15}$$

to establish the trivial solution $c = N$, with each object of the dataset forming a cluster on its own. Thus, the optimal number of cluster is found when CS is maximised, which implies minimising the intra-cluster distance (a_{pj}) while maximising the inter-cluster distance (b_{pj}) (Campello & Hruschka, 2006).

Fuzzy Silhouette (FS)

The CS index neglects discrimination of overlapped data clusters as it does not explicitly consider the fuzzy partition matrix. The fuzzy partition matrix $U = [u_{ij}]_{C \times N}$ is only used to apply on the dataset a crisp partition $\overline{U} = [\overline{u}_{ij}]_{C \times N}$, in particular $\overline{U}$ is such that $\overline{u}_{ij} = 1$ if $i = argmax_l\{u_{lj}\}$ and $\overline{u}_{ij} = 0$ otherwise. Thus, the CS index neglects discrimination of overlapped data clusters—even if these clusters have their own regions with higher data densities—as it does not explicitly consider the fuzzy partition matrix U on degrees to which clusters overlap (Campello & Hruschka, 2006). To that, a generalised silhouette criterion named the Fuzzy Silhouette (FS) index has been developed by Campello and Hruschka (2006) and considers the fuzzy partition matrix of each observation to detect areas with higher data densities when the dataset potentially has overlapping clusters. It is defined as

$$V_{FS} = \frac{\sum_{j=1}^{N} (u_{cj} - u_{qj})^\alpha s_j}{\sum_{j=1}^{N} (u_{cj} - u_{qj})^\alpha} \tag{3.16}$$

Table 3.10 FCM and PAM validation procedure

Step
Step 1: Initialise the parameters of the algorithm, except for the number of clusters, c
Step 2: Run the algorithms for different values of c's over the range $c = 2, 3, ..., c_{max}$, where $c_{max} = 15$
Step 3: Compute the validity index for each partition (U, V) obtained from step 2
Step 4: Choose the optimal partition and the optimal c according to the criteria

where s_j is the silhouette of the object j according to Eq. (3.14), u_{cj} and u_{qj} are the first and second largest elements of the jth column of the fuzzy partition matrix and $\alpha \geqslant 0$ is a weighting coefficient. Campello and Hruschka (2006) remark that Eq. (3.16) differs from Eq. (3.15) for being a weighted average of the individual silhouettes given by Eq. (3.14). As Campello and Hruschka (2006) explain "the weight of each term is determined by the difference between the membership degrees of the corresponding object to its first and second best matching fuzzy clusters, respectively. This way, an object in the near region of a cluster prototype is given more importance than another object located in an overlapping area".

Analysis of the Validation Results

Table 3.10 outlines the steps of the validation procedure used to determine the optimal partition and optimal number of clusters. The input dataset has $n = 391$ observations and $p = 6$ dimensions (see Table 3.5). The validation procedure applies Fuzzy C-means (FCM) with Euclidean and Manhattan distances and fuzzy Partitioning Around Medoids (PAM) with additional Mahalanobis distance.

The validation indexes were calculated using the R package "fclust".[7] The results of the FCM validation procedure are displayed in Table 3.11 and PAM in Table 3.12. There are no explicit guidelines on choosing optimal number of clusters based on indexes values. As it can be seen from Tables 3.11 and 3.12, not all indexes agree on the same number of clusters, and therefore, the value of optimal number of clusters was selected on the agreed majority of indexes. Highlighted in bold is the optimal value of c selected by each index according to its criteria mentioned in Table 3.9.

For FCM with Euclidean distance, PC, MPC, CS and PE indexes agree on $c = 2$ clusters, while FS and MPC suggest $c = 15$ clusters. The results of PC, PE and CS of FCM with Manhattan distance show $c = 2$ clusters is the best cluster number estimate. However, MPC calculated $c = 6$ clusters, XBI—13, FS—15. In addition, indexes CS and FS produced *not a number* (NaN) values for FCM Euclidean with $c = 13$ and 14 and FCM Manhattan with $c = 8, 9$ and 11 clusters. After the inspection of the clustering results with this number of cluster centroids, it was discovered that the FCM algorithm with both distances produces cluster centroids with equal values.

---

[7] https://cran.r-project.org/web/packages/fclust/index.html.

Table 3.11 Cluster validation of FCM clustering algorithms

Index	2	3	4	5	6	7	8	9	10	11	12	13	14	15
	FCM with Euclidean norm[1], $m = 2$, $\epsilon = 0.001$, $T = 100$, $V_0 = c$ randomly chosen[2]													
V_{PC}	**0.77**	0.64	0.57	0.54	0.53	0.52	0.55	0.54	0.56	0.58	0.59	0.57	0.57	0.60
V_{PE}	**0.36**	0.61	0.80	0.91	0.99	1.07	1.04	1.09	1.09	1.06	1.08	1.16	1.19	1.12
V_{MPC}	0.54	0.46	0.43	0.43	0.44	0.44	0.49	0.49	0.51	0.54	0.55	0.53	0.53	**0.57**
V_{CS}	**0.62**	0.52	0.44	0.46	0.51	0.52	0.50	0.48	0.52	0.56	0.56	NaN	NaN	0.55
V_{FS}	0.73	0.74	0.77	0.77	0.77	0.79	0.77	0.77	**0.80**	0.79	**0.80**	NaN	NaN	**0.80**
V_{XBI}	**0.16**	0.30	0.77	1.56	0.40	0.48	0.80	10.54	122.06	0.19	5.81	*	**	641
Index	2	3	4	5	6	7	8	9	10	11	12	13	14	15
	FCM with Manhattan norm[1], $m = 2$, $\epsilon = 0.001$, $T = 100$, $V_0 = c$ randomly chosen[2]													
V_{PC}	**0.73**	0.64	0.58	0.56	0.59	0.57	0.27	0.25	0.50	0.17	0.52	0.52	0.48	0.45
V_{PE}	**0.40**	0.61	0.78	0.89	0.88	0.96	1.64	1.77	1.24	2.06	1.28	1.29	1.44	1.54
V_{MPC}	0.46	0.46	0.44	0.45	**0.50**	0.49	0.17	0.15	0.45	0.09	0.47	0.49	0.44	0.42
V_{CS}	**0.60**	0.43	0.41	0.43	0.46	0.47	NaN	NaN	0.46	NaN	0.44	0.43	0.42	0.44
V_{FS}	0.75	0.65	0.64	0.69	0.71	0.74	NaN	NaN	0.77	NaN	0.73	0.69	0.65	**0.79**
V_{XB}	0.13	0.15	0.25	0.32	0.27	0.22	Inf	Inf	0.14	Inf	0.55	**0.12**	0.25	0.45

(1) Algorithm run with *cmeans()* function of package "*e1071*"
(2) c is the number of clusters displayed in columns
(3) * 57747.10
(4) ** 32277.93

Table 3.12 Cluster validation of PAM clustering algorithms

PAM with Euclidean norm[1], $c_{max} = 15$

Index	2	3	4	5	6	7	8	9	10	11	12	13	14	15
V_{PC}	**0.70**	0.60	0.55	0.58	0.56	0.56	0.56	0.56	0.56	0.59	0.59	0.60	0.60	0.60
V_{PE}	**0.43**	0.66	0.83	0.85	0.94	0.99	1.04	1.08	1.11	1.06	1.09	1.10	1.12	1.14
V_{MPC}	0.40	0.41	0.40	0.47	0.47	0.48	0.49	0.50	0.51	0.55	0.56	0.56	**0.57**	**0.57**
V_{CS}	**0.60**	0.42	0.45	0.43	0.45	0.46	0.47	0.50	0.54	0.55	0.57	0.57	0.57	0.58
V_{FS}	0.77	0.75	0.77	0.71	0.72	0.75	0.72	0.79	0.80	0.80	0.82	0.81	0.82	**0.83**
V_{XBI}	0.18	0.42	0.29	0.35	0.27	0.22	0.19	0.17	0.14	0.13	0.11	**0.10**	0.12	0.12

PAM with Manhattan norm[1], $c_{max} = 15$

Index	2	3	4	5	6	7	8	9	10	11	12	13	14	15
V_{PC}	**0.73**	0.64	0.60	0.57	0.59	0.57	0.58	0.59	0.60	0.60	0.60	0.61	0.61	0.61
V_{PE}	**0.40**	0.60	0.74	0.86	0.88	0.96	0.97	0.98	1.00	1.03	1.05	1.05	1.08	1.10
V_{MPC}	0.46	0.46	0.47	0.46	0.50	0.50	0.52	0.54	0.55	0.56	0.57	**0.58**	**0.58**	**0.58**
V_{CS}	**0.62**	0.41	0.43	0.47	0.46	0.49	0.50	0.52	0.53	0.54	0.55	0.54	0.55	0.56
V_{FS}	0.74	0.60	0.63	0.70	0.69	0.72	0.72	0.73	0.74	**0.76**	**0.76**	0.75	**0.76**	**0.76**
V_{XBI}	0.13	0.50	0.19	0.15	0.26	0.22	0.18	0.16	0.13	0.12	**0.11**	0.13	0.12	**0.11**

PAM with Mahalanobis norm[1], $c_{max} = 15$

Index	2	3	4	5	6	7	8	9	10	11	12	13	14	15
V_{PC}	**0.66**	0.59	0.56	0.53	0.51	0.56	0.56	0.56	0.57	0.57	0.57	0.57	0.57	0.58
V_{PE}	**0.47**	0.68	0.81	0.94	1.04	1.00	1.04	1.08	1.09	1.12	1.15	1.18	1.20	1.22
V_{MPC}	0.33	0.38	0.41	0.41	0.42	0.48	0.49	0.50	0.52	0.53	0.53	0.53	0.54	**0.55**
V_{CS}	**0.59**	0.43	0.43	0.42	0.44	0.42	0.42	0.44	0.46	0.48	0.49	0.49	0.51	0.53
V_{FS}	**0.82**	0.70	0.68	0.73	0.75	0.70	0.70	0.69	0.73	0.73	0.76	0.77	0.78	0.79
V_{XBI}	0.23	0.68	0.23	0.20	0.16	0.26	0.22	0.19	0.17	0.15	0.14	0.12	0.11	**0.10**

(1) Algorithm run with *Cluster_Medoids()* function of package "*ClusterR*"

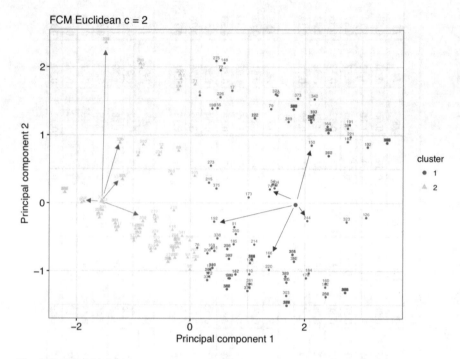

Fig. 3.13 FCM Euclidean $c = 2$

In other words, it detects two centroids at the same data point, which indicates an undistinguishable structure of the dataset. As cluster centroid values are a major parameter for CS and FS calculations, these indexes fail to perform with equal centroid coordinates. Similarly, the XBI index did not perform validation on this number of clusters producing *infinity* (Inf) value. This behaviour demonstrates the incapability of FCM algorithm to find valid partitions (separate and compact) with this number of c clusters. In contrast, PAM clustering has succeeded at detecting the structure in the data by producing valid values of indexes. This could be due to the fact that PAM considers initial cluster centroids from the given dataset and not calculated as artificial objects (weighted means) as is the case with FCM. According to the agreement of PC, PE, CS and FS, the optimal of $c = 2$ is found for PAM with Euclidean, Manhattan and Mahalanobis distances; however, MPC, FS and XBI also indicated the best partition with $c = 15$.

To visualise the suggested partitions, the plots presented in this section are produced with the help of *fviz_cluster()* function of the *R* package *factoextra*.[8] The visualisation is based on two dimensions, where the fviz_cluster() function conducts *principle component analysis* (Smith, 2002) of the given dataset and plots its first two principle components on x and y axes of the plot. Figure 3.13 illustrates

---

[8] https://cran.r-project.org/web/packages/factoextra/factoextra.pdf.

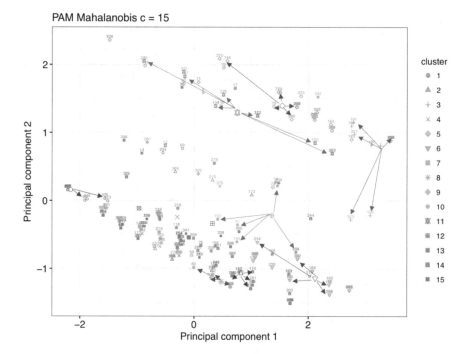

Fig. 3.14 PAM Mahalanobis $c = 15$

the partition dataset of the FCM Euclidean with $c = 2$ as per the suggested valid values of indexes. As observed, a 2-cluster solution can potentially provide a good separation of clusters, and however, the compactness is drastically low.

Figure 3.14 displays a 15-cluster solution as produced by the PAM Mahalanobis algorithm. It can be observed that the compactness of clusters is partially improved, whereas the separation of cluster centroids significantly suffers. For example, clusters 1, 6, 8 and 14 are small and compact, and however, they hardly separate with other neighbouring clusters, whereas cluster 11 is distinctively separated, but its data points are weakly compacted. It is interesting to note that while the FCM algorithm tends to produce only spherical clusters, PAM produces spherical clusters like 3 and 10, as well as more ellipsoidal clusters like 8 and 11.

In general, the proposed optimal number of clusters unfortunately does not retain both properties of compactness and separation of produced partition. This could be due to the following reasons: one is the nature of the given dataset and the lack of its structure. It seems that privacy profiles tend to be indistinctive, and dataset dimensions are highly correlated among each other (see Table 3.6). To that, Pal and Bezdek (1995) suggest that "the unique minimum V_{PC} (or maximum V_{PE}) are very helpful in deciding when the structure is not being found." In our dataset, the proposed validity index values of $c = 2$ or 15 clusters do not provide useful information, which indicates a vague structure and hardly distinguishable observations in the dataset. Therefore, the min(PC), min(MPC) and max(PE) values

Table 3.13 Results of cluster validity indexes for optimal N of clusters

Distance	Euclidean	Manhattan	Mahalanobis
Algorithm			
FCM	2, 15, **4, 5, 7**	2, 6, 13, 15	x
PAM	2, 15, **4**	2, 15, **3, 5, 6**	2, 15, **6**

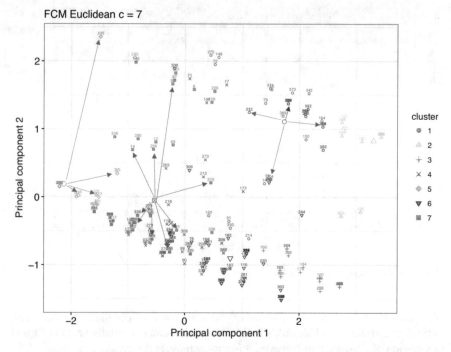

Fig. 3.15 PAM Mahalanobis $c = 7$

are observed. As a result, the max(PE) values always tend to the maximum number of clusters which does not support obtaining meaningful classifications. The min(PC) indicated for FCM Euclidean $c = 7$, FCM Manhattan $c = 11$, PAM Euclidean $c = 4$, PAM Manhattan $c = 5$ and 7 and PAM Mahalanobis $c = 6$ (indicated in bold in Table 3.13). According to that, Figs. 3.15 and 3.16 display visualisations of FCM Euclidean with 7 clusters and PAM Mahalanobis with 6 clusters as the most differentiated partition representation among other suggestions as produced by a min(PC). It can be seen that, when compared to a 2-cluster solution, the FCM Euclidean with 7 clusters produced more compact clusters like 3, 4 and 6, and however, there are still clusters with low compactness but higher separation, for instance, clusters 1, 5 and 7. PAM Mahalanobis with 6 clusters partitioned more compact ellipsoidal clusters as 2, 3, 4 and 6, where cluster 3 is the most separate one. Clusters 1 and 5 have the spherical form with low compactness and separation from other clusters. It can be concluded that with the given dataset of privacy profiles, it is hard to find a balance between compactness and separation

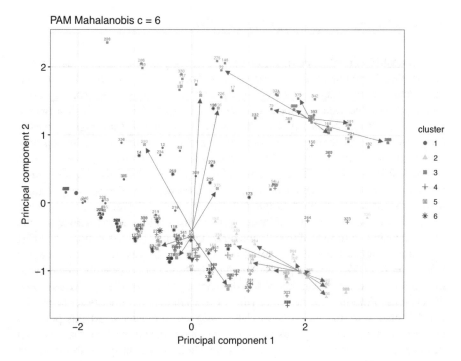

Fig. 3.16 PAM Mahalanobis $c = 6$

of clusters while trying to produce a meaningful classification. To that, another possible reason can be related to the imperfect performance of the chosen clustering algorithms. Both algorithms, FCM and PAM, try to find hyper spherical shapes of clusters, whereas, if to observe the visualisation of data points in the presented plots, a possible three well-separated ellipsoidal shapes can be distinguished. Only PAM as a consequence of the calculation of covariance between variables in the Mahalanobis distance formula succeeded to detect some of the existing ellipsoidal forms in the dataset (see Fig. 3.16, e.g., yellow cluster 2 and grey cluster 3). The behaviour of searching ellipsoidal forms is a characteristic of the Gustafson–Kessel clustering algorithm (Gustafson & Kessel, 1979). Using different clustering approaches with different distance measures is intentionally performed to further use this information for recommendation calculation. Visualisation of clustering results presented the difference in cluster results, and therefore, the next section describes in detail the characteristics of fuzzy privacy profiles.

3.3.3   Discussion of Fuzzy Privacy Profiles

To demonstrate the characteristics of fuzzy privacy profiles, Fig. 3.17 depicts the vector of each calculated *cluster centroid* (based on FCM Euclidean with 4 clusters) and vectors of *three user privacy profiles*. The axes of the radar chart represent data types and the values of axes represent a sharing decision of this data type to an audience. It can be clearly seen that users in the *cluster 1* are highly privacy-preserved and keep their profile's data types private and unshared, allowing only friends the possibility to contact them. In contrast, in *cluster 4* users' privacy profiles distinguished as totally public, whereas *clusters 3 and 2* have users with various privacy preferences per each data type. Users in *cluster 3* set their privacy settings to friends for most of the data types. Users in *cluster 2* prefer to keep private personal information and vote intention private, their relations and activity on the platform visible to friends of friends and other dataset up visible to public. The FCM algorithm assigned *user-181* to the cluster 4 with the highest membership degree value $m = 0.99$. The privacy profile vector of the user-181 is perfectly aligned with the vector of the corresponding centroid, meaning that user-181 agrees across all dimensions with cluster 4 centroid, which has visibility preferences set to public. On the other side, the *user-139* was also assigned to cluster 4. At this point, in the case of traditional sharp clustering, we only have this information that user-139 belongs to this cluster. However, the beneficial side of the fuzzy clustering is that it provides additional information, such that user-139 belongs to the cluster 4 with the highest membership degree of $m = 0.36$, but he also attains similarity to the cluster 2 with the membership degree of $m = 0.27$, to cluster 3 with $m = 0.24$ and to cluster 1 with $m = 0.13$.

This is a genuine example of the multidimensional privacy profile, where 50% of users' privacy decisions agreed with the sharply assigned cluster centroid. Thus, the classification of this user is in a gradual manner to all clusters. As seen from the user-139 privacy profile, he does not agree with cluster 4 on the privacy decision related to "MyActivity". In that case, cluster 4 would suggest opening this data to the public, whereas cluster 2 would recommend opening it only to friends of friends. Moreover, cluster 2 has more restrictive visibility preferences with regard to "VoteIntention" data type compared to the initial user's privacy decision. Based on that, one privacy suggestion might be that user-139 can be recommended either to share "MyActivity" data to public according to cluster 1 or to restrict "VoteIntention" to be visible only to friends, according to cluster 2. Another example includes the *user-12* privacy profile vector which has been assigned to cluster 4 with the highest membership degree of $m = 0.33$, and it also belongs to the cluster 2 with degree of $m = 0.28$ and cluster 3 with $m = 0.26$. The graph of user-12 indicates that it does not totally agree with the centroid cluster 4, but the user agrees with cluster 2 on MyRelations visibility and with cluster 3 on data related to Contact sharing decision. However, not all profiles possess such characteristics, for instance, user-181 has a multidimensional profile, but his privacy decisions are similar across all dimensions.

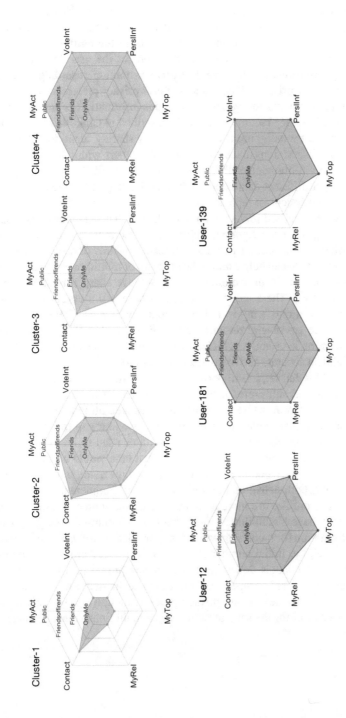

Fig. 3.17 Cluster centroids and users' privacy profile vectors

Having additional insights on users' privacy preferences gives more options for the design of privacy suggestions as well as increasing its precision. Using sharp classification, saying, for example, that users in the *cluster-4* are "privacy liberals", in our case makes an exact classification for the *user-181*; however, it simultaneously discriminates the *user-139* privacy opinion regarding other data types, which are more private. Thus, nuances of user privacy preferences can be well detected with the fuzzy clustering. How to use this information as an advantage to personalisation of privacy recommendation is described in Chap. 4. The associated risks may increase by assigning a class label on a sharply identified cluster and neglecting those observations that differentiate from others within that cluster. This demonstrates the multidimensionality of user privacy profiles where user privacy decision varies per different data item. To this, the fuzzy partitioning of the dataset may produce a more accurate representation of clusters which can possibly help to calculate more personalised privacy recommendations. The advantageous property of fuzzy clustering is that it assigns a membership degree value for each observation, showing to what extent the user possesses intrinsic features of each cluster in the dataset. This advantage can help capture the problem of multidimensionality of user privacy profiles and assist in avoiding a discriminative sharp classification (e.g., user-12 and user-139). There are few studies that observed users' privacy profiles with the support of a clustering technique (Knijnenburg et al., 2013; Wisniewski et al., 2017). There are several reasons for this, firstly, as the clustering technique is a type of machine learning, a sufficient data of user privacy profiles needs to be obtained to build an accurate and robust user privacy model. Also, when considering user privacy profiles dataset, it is important to make a differentiation between users' privacy settings and privacy preferences. The former represents users' actual privacy behaviour on the platform, while the latter expresses their attitude for privacy and, in this case, is important to consider the attitude–behaviour gap (privacy paradox) to avoid fallacious models. Secondly, privacy profiles used to be examined from the unidimensional representation. Clustering in that case would be sufficient, and however, it might produce poorer results and lead to an oversimplification of users' privacy behaviour, both actual and attitudinal. To that, Knijnenburg et al. (2013) stated that privacy profiles are more than unidimensional representation where, on the contrary, they have a multidimensional structure. Multidimensionality provides additional information for modelling user privacy profiles. Thirdly, depending on the dataset, most often the initial number of clusters for privacy profiles is unknown. Assigning the cluster labels downgrades the privacy profile to a unidimensional representation. Therefore, unsupervised clustering technique will be relevant to observe existing tendencies among privacy profiles, though without relating to a particular cluster label for the sake of preserving a multidimensional characteristic of the profile.

3.4   User Evaluation of Privacy Behaviour

Lederer et al. (2004) state that existing systems still make it difficult for people
to manage their privacy, and designs of these systems inhibit people's abilities
to both understand the privacy implications of their use and conduct socially
meaningful actions through them. When confronted with a realistic description of a
privacy scenario, users' disclosure preferences differ from what they had previously
considered they would be, which is a vivid example of privacy paradox.[9]

This section is dedicated to the evaluation of users' privacy behaviours on the
Participa Inteligente platform to understand if there was a privacy paradox effect
if users' actual behaviour diverge with initial privacy attitudes and the reasons
behind using default settings. The evaluation framework displayed in Fig. 3.18
addresses users' experience (EXP) of using privacy management tool (OSA) which
allowed to set up privacy settings for users' profiles. In particular, if the users had
default privacy settings—was it set as an actual privacy preference, or it is only
the intention. The underlying reasons of having default settings are explored by the
possible effect of lack of knowledge (how to use privacy settings) or simply by
forgetting to change default privacy settings. If the user did not use default privacy
settings, it is evaluated how frequently the user changed her privacy settings and
if it was easy to use the privacy management tool for that. Additionally, a possible
effect of users' personal characteristics on their privacy behaviour is investigated.
The next sections describe in detail every aspect of this framework.

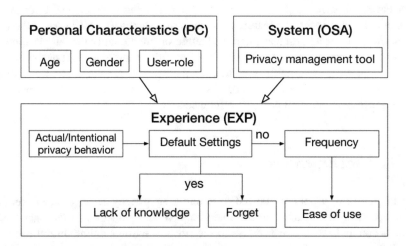

Fig. 3.18 Evaluation framework of user privacy behaviours

---

[9] More information on privacy paradox is in Chap. 2.

3.4.1   Objective System Aspect

Privacy controls provided by online platforms are heavily underexploited by users. Previous research showed that users are less likely to change default privacy settings (Gross & Acquisti, 2005), while more recent research demonstrate that users tend to change default settings to a reasonable extent (Dey et al., 2012; Stutzman et al., 2012). Different factors could distance users from changing their default privacy settings. One of the issues is the complexity of privacy controls, so that users are having troubles correctly configuring their privacy settings. For example, the lack of a user-friendly design indicated to be a major problem in making privacy controls work and demonstrated that "users are overtaxed with existing privacy schemes" (Reinhardt et al., 2015).

The design of the privacy management tool on the platform potentially creates limitations and barriers for expressing one's privacy preferences. It may define the extent of privacy users can have on the platform and influence user's experience with their privacy. On the Participa Intelligente (PI) platform, the privacy management tool was developed according to the user privacy profile framework mentioned in Fig. 3.5. In the dataset form, it represents a sharing matrix (see Tables 3.2 and 3.5), where the rows of the matrix represent users, the columns represent data types and the cell values indicate the defined sharing decision of the data to a particular audience. However, privacy behaviours can go beyond the simple sharing matrix and can be defined through more complex schemas. For example, Wisniewski et al. (2017) investigated user privacy behaviours in terms of features and settings that Facebook users apply as mechanism for managing interpersonal boundaries. The authors also identified feature awareness that shows to which degree the user knows/recognises a particular interface feature or functionality that allows them to perform a particular privacy task. This is a very important factor as it determines to what extent users are capable of addressing their privacy. In our study, we evaluate how the *privacy management tool* deployed on the platform affects user experience when expressing personal privacy preferences.

3.4.2   User Experience

On PI platform, users are allowed to define their privacy settings when creating their account. In addition, on the main page of the platform, users logged into their accounts have a direct access to the privacy settings configuration page. In PI platform, privacy settings are set up by default to "public" visibility. Therefore, the disadvantage of the current privacy management tool is that it is not possible to identify whether the *default settings* were left unchanged by users' personal intention by simply skipping this step or probably did not understand how to use this functionality and, later, simply forget to change their privacy settings.

The reason for the "defaultism" tendency may be caused by the "privacy paradox" effect, for example, when a user with a high privacy concern attitude leaves default settings unchanged which uncover her data to all users on the platform. Even though being a privacy concerned person, the user's actual privacy behaviour diverges with his initial privacy attitudes. Justifying reasons for the "defaultism" tendency in configuring privacy settings can be related to the feature awareness of the current privacy management tool, in other words, due to the user's *lack of knowledge* on privacy management on the platform. Young and Quan-Haase (2009) reported that students are often unaware, or have forgotten, what information they have disclosed and what privacy settings they have activated. In addition, Acquisti and Gross (2006) stated that the majority of Facebook users realise the true visibility of their profiles; however, the significant minority of users are still underestimating the visibility borderlines of their profiles.

Studies of Sawaya et al. (2017), Kang et al. (2015) show that knowledge on computer security does not necessarily, in reality, lead people to behave more securely or that it is not the main factor driving actual computer security behaviour. Similar to users' disclosure behaviour, knowing how to change your privacy settings will not substantially affect your actual disclosure behaviour. Therefore, we want to investigate if users used default settings as they were unaware of how to use the privacy management tool on the platform; if not, was the other reason of using default settings because they just *forgot* to change them. Also, for those users who had actually configured their privacy settings on the platform, we wanted to know how often a user changed his profile privacy settings (*frequency*). To that, the user interface plays an important role if users were easily able to configure their privacy preferences (*ease of use*).

3.4.3 Personal Characteristics

Personal user characteristics may have an effect on the user's experience in regard to the privacy management tool. Quercia et al. (2012) reported that men are more likely to publicly share privacy-sensitive fields. Moreover, even if both genders share an equal amount of private information, only men tend to expand the visibility beyond their social circles. In addition, Hoy and Milne (2010) showed that women are more likely to undertake proactive self-protective behaviours and believe that it is important to be knowledgeable on the use of their personal information. However, studies of Yao et al. (2007) and Sawaya et al. (2017) demonstrate that gender has no direct or indirect impact on privacy concerns on online platforms and on actual privacy behaviour. As the aforementioned studies provide conflicting results with regard to gender effect on privacy concerns and behaviour, in our evaluation, we will investigate if the effect of *gender* occurred on our platform. Additionally, in the study by Cho et al. (2009), he showed that older female users were more concerned with online privacy than their younger, male counterparts. Therefore, the *age* of users can have an effect on their privacy behaviours, and thus, it is also included in our evaluation model.

Similar to gender, the culture of users affects the various visibility tendency of privacy profiles. Studies report that online users from individualistic countries express higher privacy concerns, while users from collectivistic countries are likely to exhibit less private behaviour online and to be less concerned about online privacy. Moreover, the cultural variability may be one of the reasons for the existence of the privacy paradox (Cho et al., 2009; Li et al., 2017; Sawaya et al., 2017). The users in our study are representatives of a single nationality, which is represented by citizens of Ecuador. Therefore, the *culture* factor is included in the framework; however, it has no comparative evaluation. In addition, users on PI platform can be differentiated by two roles: voters and political members. The majority of users are represented by voters, while only six users are representatives of political parties. The *user-role* on platforms have a substantial effect on privacy behaviours. As the number of users from political parties is significantly less than voters, the user-role factor is included in the evaluation framework but not considered for further analysis.

3.4.4   Evaluation Analysis

The user evaluation is conducted in a form of an online survey. The survey commenced on 5 June 2017 and ended on 31 July 2017. The questions related to our evaluation framework are outlined in Sect. B.1, Table B.1. The dataset of collected user responses consists of 67 users' answers. Among them, 19 females, 47 males and 1 user did not provide gender information. The age is between 23 and 39 years old (median age is 31). Among those users, 61 are citizens and 6 are representatives of the political party (Table B.1). The minimum time used to answer all questions was 18.44 seconds and the maximum time was 324.22 s (mean 53.19 s).

Independent Variables Analysis

As the survey questions were presented as a guided structure, the resulted dataset is underpowered and does not have significant inferences. However, among those insignificant results, there are some interesting observations worth discussing. The chi-square test and t-test (bootstrapping) were run on the dataset. As the data sample is small, we used values of chi-square test with Yates' continuity corrections. Among all insignificant relations, we will shortly discuss the relations that inferred the significance values of Pearson's chi-square test with Yates' continuity corrections with significance values *at least p<0.3* (Fig. 3.19).

There was a significant association between actual privacy behaviour and user's forgetting tendency to change privacy settings with $X^2(1) = 3.86$, $p < 0.05$. The odds of users having default privacy settings as they forgot to change it were

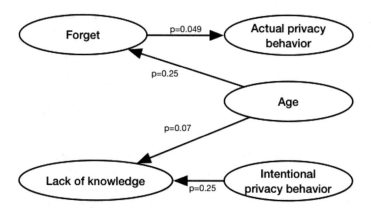

Fig. 3.19 Relations between variables with $p < 0.3$

4.857 times higher than users having default privacy setting intentionally (i.e., they did not forget to change them) (95% CI: [1.007006, 24.68733]). This significant finding reflects that when users do forget to change privacy settings approximately 77.27% of users' accounts have default privacy settings and 22.72% do not, whereas when users do not forget to change privacy settings, only 58.82% are without default settings and 41.17% of users stay with default settings. *Therefore, we can conclude that people who use default privacy settings mostly do so as they simply forget to change their privacy settings. However, even if some users do not forget to change privacy settings, there are some who prefer to stay with the default settings.* The relation between users' attitude privacy behaviour and their knowledge on how to change privacy settings displayed an association with $X^2(1) = 1.284108$, $p = 0.2571366$. Among users who did not know how to change privacy settings, 75% were with a negative attitude of having a public privacy setting, while only 25% were with a positive attitude of being public. Moreover, those users who knew where/how to change privacy settings were almost equally represented by both groups (47.059% positive to be public against 52.941%). This, actually, looks quite unexpected as we tend to assume that those people who care about privacy, according to their attitudes, surely tend to know where/how to change the privacy settings (could be related to "privacy paradox" effect, such as—"I care about my privacy, but I don't make an effort to figure out how to change my default privacy settings."). *Thus, it was not found that knowing how to change privacy settings was substantially affected by the user's disclosure behaviour intentions.*

The findings also showed that age has, although insignificant, some effect on variables such as knowledge and tendency to forget changing default settings. On average users who did not know how to change privacy settings tend to be 9 years younger than users who know how to change defaults settings. This difference was not significant $t(39.989) = -1.83$, $p = 0.075$; however, it represents almost a medium-size effect $r = 0.277$. Less significantly, compared to knowledge, the age has an effect on users' forgetting tendency. On average older users did not forget to

Fig. 3.20 Relation between
combined variable and
knowledge

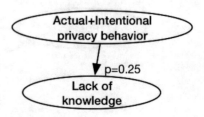

change their default privacy settings, while their younger counterparts tend to forget.
The difference was not significant $t(32.285) = 1.17$, $p = 0.252$, and it represents
a small-size effect $r = 0.201$. Based on those findings, it is assumed that the older
the user the more carefully she approaches the configuration of privacy settings.

Combined Variable Analysis

For further analysis, we have created a combined variable which reflects if
user's privacy behaviour is consistent or not (Fig. 3.20). The variable combines
the actual privacy behaviour and attitude privacy behaviour values. This variable can be represented in two conditions: first—consistent privacy behaviour
(Q1&Q4=Yes AND Q1&Q4=No) and second—inconsistent privacy behaviour
(Q1=Yes&Q4=No AND Q1=No&Q4=Yes).

There is an insignificant association between users' consistent privacy behaviour
and knowledge on privacy settings with $X^2(1) = 1.284108$, $p = 0.25$. Among
those users who knew how to change privacy settings, 8 users had consistent
privacy behaviour, while 9 users were inconsistent. Not surprisingly, among users
who did not know how to change privacy settings, the majority (75%) were users
with inconsistent privacy behaviours against users with consistent behaviours of
42.8%. This result may possibly conclude that as more users are consistent with
their privacy behaviour, they generally tend to figure out how to change default
privacy settings, while users with inconsistent behaviours are mostly unaware about
privacy settings on the platform. Both groups of people, consistent and inconsistent,
found the privacy management tool neutrally easy to use. However, those who
disagreed with the ease of use (6 out of 7 users) were reported by users with
inconsistent privacy behaviours. The time spent to answer the survey has also been
used to analyse the population. We found that, on average, people with consistent
behaviours ($M = 61.26$ sec) spend 19 seconds more answering the survey questions
than people with inconsistent behaviours ($M = 46.99$ sec).

3.5   Conclusions

To conclude the preliminary user evaluation, the actual use of the default settings
might be explained by people's forgetting tendency to change default settings. We
might expect that user's knowledge (feature awareness) about privacy settings can

be explained by their privacy concerns (e.g., people with high privacy concerns might know how to change privacy settings), and however the preliminary results showed the opposite—people with protective privacy attitudes still did not know how to use privacy settings. However, knowledge can be explained by the user's consistent privacy behaviour. Age seems to play an important role on users' knowledge and the tendency to forget to change initial privacy settings. Users with consistent behaviours considered the survey more carefully by taking more time to answer questions rather than inconsistent users. It must be taken into account that these results cannot be generalised because they are affected by two other context variables: it is focused on the one culture representatives (citizens of Ecuador), and the platform context relates to the political participation which also affects users disclosure behaviour. Based on the results of this study, it can be shown that users need a privacy decision support in a form of a privacy recommendations.

References

Acquisti, A., & Gross, R. (2006). Imagined communities: Awareness, information sharing, and privacy on the Facebook. In *International workshop on privacy enhancing technologies*, (pp. 36–58). Springer.

Aïmeur, E., Gambs, S., & H, A. (2009). UPP: User privacy policy for social networking sites. In *2009 Fourth international conference on internet and web applications and services*.

Altman, I. (1977). Privacy regulation: Culturally universal or culturally specific? *Journal of Social Issues, 33*(3), 66–84.

Bezdek, J. C. (1974). Cluster validity with fuzzy sets. *Journal of Cybernetics, 3*(3), 58–73.

Bezdek, J., & Hathaway, R. (2002). VAT: A tool for visual assessment of (cluster) tendency. In *IJCNN* (pp. 2225–2230).

Bezdek, J. C., Ehrlich, R., & Full, W. (1984). FCM: The fuzzy c-means clustering algorithm. *Computers and Geosciences, 10*(2–3), 191–203.

Campello, R. J., & Hruschka, E. R. (2006). A fuzzy extension of the silhouette width criterion for cluster analysis. *Fuzzy Sets and Systems, 157*(21), 2858–2875.

Cho, H., Rivera-Sánchez, M., & Lim, S. S. (2009). A multinational study on online privacy: global concerns and local responses. *New Media & Society, 11*(3), 395–416.

Dave, R. N. (1996). Validating fuzzy partitions obtained through c-shells clustering. *Pattern Recognition Letters, 17*(6), 613–623.

Dey, R., Jelveh, Z., & Ross, K. (2012). Facebook users have become much more private: A large-scale study. In *2012 IEEE International conference on pervasive computing and communications workshops (PERCOM workshops)* (pp. 346–352). IEEE.

Dunn, J. C. (1973). A fuzzy relative of the ISODATA process and its use in detecting compact well-separated clusters. *Journal of Cybernetics, 3*(3), 32–57.

Fang, L., & LeFevre, K. (2010). Privacy wizards for social networking sites. In *Proceedings of the 19th international conference on world wide web*.

Fivaz, J., & Schwarz, D. (2007). Nailing the pudding to the wall–e-democracy as catalyst for transparency and accountability. In *International conference on direct democracy in Latin America* (pp. 14–15).

Garzia, D., & Marschall, S. (2012). Voting advice applications under review: the state of research. *International Journal of Electronic Governance, 5*(3–4), 203–222.

Giordani, P., & Ferraro, M. B. (2015). Package 'fclust': fuzzy clustering. CRAN R studio.

Gross, R., & Acquisti, A. (2005). Information revelation and privacy in online social networks. In *Proceedings of the 2005 ACM workshop on privacy in the electronic society* (pp. 71–80).

Gustafson, D. E., & Kessel, W. C. (1979). Fuzzy clustering with a fuzzy covariance matrix. In *1978 IEEE conference on decision and control including the 17th symposium on adaptive processes* (pp. 761–766). IEEE.

Hoy, M. G., & Milne, G. (2010). Gender differences in privacy-related measures for young adult Facebook users. *Journal of Interactive Advertising, 10*(2), 28–45.

Huang, Z. (1997). A fast clustering algorithm to cluster very large categorical data sets in data mining. *DMKD, 3*(8), 34–39.

Huckfeldt, R., & Sprague, J. (1987). Networks in context: The social flow of political information. *American Political Science Review, 81*(4), 1197–1216.

Jiu-Lun Fan, C.-M. W., & Ma, Y.-L. (2000). A modified partition coefficient. In *Signal Processing Proceedings* (vol. 3, pp. 1496–1499). IEEE.

Johnson, M., Egelman, S., & Bellovin, S. M. (2012). Facebook and privacy: It's complicated. In *Proceedings of the eighth symposium on usable privacy and security*.

Kang, R., Dabbish, L., Fruchter, N., & Kiesler, S. (2015). My data just goes everywhere? User mental models of the internet and implications for privacy and security. In *Symposium on usable privacy and security (SOUPS)* (pp. 39–52). USENIX Association Berkeley, CA.

Kaskina, A. (2018). Exploring nuances of user privacy preferences on a platform for political participation. In *2018 International conference on eDemocracy & eGovernment (ICEDEG)* (pp. 89–94). IEEE.

Kaskina, A., & Meier, A. (2016). Integrating privacy and trust in voting advice applications. In *Third international conference on eDemocracy & eGovernment (ICEDEG)* (pp. 20–25). IEEE.

Kaskina, A., & Radovanovic, N. (2016). How to build trust-aware voting advice applications? In *International conference on electronic government and the information systems perspective* (pp. 48–61). Springer.

Katakis, I., Tsapatsoulis, N., Mendez, F., Triga, V., & Djouvas, C. (2014). Social voting advice applications – definitions, challenges, datasets and evaluation. *IEEE Transactions on Cybernetics, 44*(7), 1039–1052.

Kaufman, L., & Rousseeuw, P. J. (2009). *Finding groups in data: An introduction to cluster analysis* (vol. 344). John Wiley & Sons.

Kim, Y. (2011). The contribution of social network sites to exposure to political difference: The relationships among SNSS, online political messaging, and exposure to cross-cutting perspectives. *Computers in Human Behavior, 27*(2), 971–977.

Kim, D.-W., Lee, K. H., & Lee, D. (2004). On cluster validity index for estimation of the optimal number of fuzzy clusters. *Pattern Recognition, 37*(10), 2009–2025.

Knijnenburg, B. P. (2017). Privacy? i can't even! making a case for user-tailored privacy. *IEEE Security & Privacy, 15*(4), 62–67.

Knijnenburg, B. P., & Kobsa, A. (2013). Making decisions about privacy: Information disclosure in context-aware recommneder systems. *ACM Transactions on Interactive Intelligent Systems, 3*(3), 1–23.

Knijnenburg, B., Kobsa, A., & Jin, H. (2013). Dimensionality of information disclosure behavior. *Journal of Human-Computer Studies, 71*(12), 1144–1162.

Kobsa, A. (2001). Tailoring privacy to users' needs. In *International conference on user modeling* (pp. 301–313). Springer.

Krasnova, H., Günther, O., Spiekermann, S., & Koroleva, K. (2009). Privacy concerns and identity in online social networks. *Identity in the Information Society, 2*(1), 39–63.

Kwon, K. H., Moon, S.-I., & Stefanone, M. A. (2015). Unspeaking on Facebook? Testing network effects on self-censorship of political expressions in social network sites. *Quality & Quantity, 49*(4), 1417–1435.

Ladner, A., & Meier, A. (2014). Digitale politische Partizipation-Spannungsfeld zwischen MyPolitics und OurPolitics. *HMD Praxis der Wirtschaftsinformatik, 51*(6), 867–882.

Lederer, S., Hong, J. I., Dey, A. K., & Landay, J. A. (2004). Personal privacy through understanding and action: five pitfalls for designers. *Personal and Ubiquitous Computing, 8*(6), 440–454.

Li, Y., Kobsa, A., Knijnenburg, B. P., Nguyen, C., et al. (2017). Cross-cultural privacy prediction. *Proceedings on Privacy Enhancing Technologies, 2017*(2), 113–132.

Liu, K., & Terzi, E. (2010). A framework for computing the privacy scores of users in online social networks. *ACM Transactions on Knowledge Discovery from Data (TKDD), 5*(1), 6.

Meier, A. (2012). *eDemocracy and eGovernment: Stages of a democratic knowledge society.* Springer-Verlag, Berlin, Heidelberg.

Meier, A., Kaskina, A., & Teran, L. (2018). Politische Partizipation–eSociety anders gedacht. *HMD Praxis der Wirtschaftsinformatik* (pp. 1–13).

Munemasa, T., & Iwaihara, M. (2011). Trend analysis and recommendation of users? Privacy settings on social networking services. In *International conference on social informatics* (pp. 184–197). Springer.

Pal, N. R., & Bezdek, J. C. (1995). On cluster validity for the fuzzy c-means model. In *IEEE transactions on fuzzy systems* (vol. 3). IEEE.

Portmann, E. (2012). *The FORA framework: A fuzzy grassroots ontology for online reputation management.* Springer Science & Business Media.

Quercia, D., Casas, D. L., J.P. Pesce, D. S., Kosinski, M., Almeida, V., & Crowcroft (2012). Facebook and privacy: The balancing act of personality, gender, and relationship currency. In *ICWSM.*

Reinhardt, D., Engelmann, F., & Hollick, M. (2015). Can I help you setting your privacy? A survey-based exploration of users' attitudes towards privacy suggestions. In *Proceedings of the 13th international conference on advances in mobile computing and multimedia* (pp. 347–356). ACM.

Rokach, L., & Maimon, O. (2005). Clustering methods. In *Data mining and knowledge discovery handbook* (pp. 321–352). Springer.

Sawaya, Y., Sharif, M., Christin, N., Kubota, A., Nakarai, A., & Yamada, A. (2017). Self-confidence trumps knowledge: A cross-cultural study of security behavior. In *Proceedings of the 2017 CHI conference on human factors in computing systems* (pp. 2202–2214). ACM.

Smith, L. I. (2002). A tutorial on principal components analysis. Technical report.

Stutzman, F., Gross, R., & Acquisti, A. (2012). Silent listeners: The evolution of privacy and disclosure on Facebook. *Journal of Privacy and Confidentiality, 4*(2). https://doi.org/10.29012/jpc.v4i2.620.

Terán, L., & Mancera, J. (2017). Applying dynamic profiles on voting advice applications. In *Wirtschaftsinformatik in Theorie und Praxis* (pp. 153–175). Springer.

Walgrave, S., Nuytemans, M., & Pepermans, K. (2009). Voting aid applications and the effect of statement selection. *West European Politics, 32*(6), 1161–1180.

Wang, W., & Zhang, Y. (2007). On fuzzy cluster validity indices. *Fuzzy Sets and Systems, 158*(19), 2095–2117.

Westin, A. F. (1968). Privacy and freedom. *Washington and Lee Law Review, 25*(1), 166.

Wisniewski, P., Knijnenburg, B., & Lipford, H. (2017). Making privacy personal: Profiling social network users to inform privacy education and nudging. *International Journal of Human-Computer Studies, 98*, 95–108.

Wu, K.-L., & Yang, M.-S. (2005). A cluster validity index for fuzzy clustering. *Pattern Recognition Letters, 26*(9), 1275–1291.

Xie, X. L., & Beni, G. (1991). A validity measure for fuzzy clustering. *IEEE Transactions on Pattern Analysis and Machine Intelligence, 13*(8), 841–847.

Yao, M. Z., Rice, R. E., & Wallis, K. (2007). Predicting user concerns about online privacy. *Journal of the Association for Information Science and Technology, 58*(5), 710–722.

Young, A. L., & Quan-Haase, A. (2009). Information revelation and internet privacy concerns on social network sites: a case study of Facebook. In *Proceedings of the fourth international conference on communities and technologies* (pp. 265–274). ACM.

Chapter 4
Fuzzy-Based Privacy Settings Recommender System

4.1 Conceptual Development

4.1.1 Overview of the Existing Systems

Due to the fact that individuals each have a different perception on privacy concerns, it becomes complicated to find the ultimate privacy policy that fulfils all the users' needs. Previous research frameworks for privacy recommendations mostly focused on a unidimensional privacy profile representation (Munemasa & Iwaihara, 2011; Naini et al., 2015) and, in rare cases, contextualised frameworks are used where other factors including the trustworthiness of the information recipients, information sensitivity or other privacy attitudes are considered in the model (Bahirat et al., 2018; Dong et al., 2016). Presented in the following sections privacy recommender systems are described for the following reasons: the privacy wizard is the one of the earliest works on developing an automated privacy management support tool; the personalised privacy assistant system is the latest practical solution that combines results of several years of research; YourPrivacyProtector is an example of an interesting approach but with weak technical rationale.

Privacy Wizard

Fang and LeFevre (2010) proposed a privacy wizard which aims to automatically configure user's privacy settings with minimal effort from the user. The main engine of the wizard is the privacy preference model classifier which solicits data input from two parts of the system architecture: user input and feature extraction. It collects users' answers to questions related to their privacy preferences, in particular, the sharing preference of the specific data to a particular person in their social network. At the same time it extracts features from the user's neighbourhood (list of friends) structure and general profile data, such as gender, age, education, etc. In addition, their classifier model uses active learning which helps handle the limits of the user's effort to assign labels to their friends' network. Afterwards, the model was used to automatically configure user privacy settings, thus, reducing user effort. Certainly, it is important to consider the user's effort in configuring personalised privacy settings, however, in this case it was not proven, in terms of accuracy, that the relation to a user's list of friends provides adequate information. In addition, the user input for the classifier was based on the binary user answers such as "yes"; "no". The binarization of user's sharing preferences oversimplifies user privacy perceptions. Also, the authors mentioned that a manual labelling of a user's 25 friends increases the average accuracy to over 90%. A possible drawback of this system may appear with users having less privacy concerns. They may experience cognitive laziness or "configuration fatigue" by skipping the required configuration limit of settings which may, in turn, affect the accuracy of the proposed automation. Again, this can be criticised towards the additional user effort and eventually "configuration fatigue".

YourPrivacyProtector

Ghazinour et al. (2013) suggest a recommender system which aims to assist people in using their privacy settings in social media. Their system is based on defined user profiles which include attributes related to the user's personal data (name, gender, birthdate, education, etc.), their interests (movies, books, politics, etc.) and their privacy settings on photo albums. Based on this data, the system classifies user's privacy behaviour into three categories, such as "ignorant", "pragmatic" and "fundamentalist", which was proposed by Westin (1968). These behaviour categories help to understand the attitude towards privacy settings in terms of their interests and published content. Users are classified using decisions trees rules to derive user profiles based on the above-mentioned categories. Then, the system calculates recommendations using the k-nearest neighbour (KNN) algorithm. It matches similar profiles to the target user and then provides recommendations if certain information should be hidden or disclosed. In general, the proposed recommender system is based on the intuition of the collaborative filtering (Herlocker et al., 2000), where the similarity between the target user's privacy preferences and other users who share common privacy preferences is calculated. However, several critical moments can be addressed towards it. In their work, even though having the multidimensional structure of user's profiles, their model downsizes user profiles into a unidimensional categorisation which overlooks different disclosing tendencies per each data attributes. Also, the training dataset of their model is based on the binary sharing values ("disclose"; "not disclose"), which neglects the granularity of a user's sharing decision. Finally, the recommender system was missing the evaluation and justification of the optimal values of K-neighbours in the KNN-classification algorithm. Thus, this system is a demonstrative example of a sharp classification of users' privacy profiles.

Personalised Privacy Assistant

Recent work of Liu et al. (2016) presents a personalised privacy assistant (PPA) which facilitates a users' privacy permissions management for mobile applications. The privacy permission settings for mobile application allow the decision to allow or deny third party application access to data stored on a user's mobile device. Granting permissions to third parties also relates to privacy issues. In this way, the PPA's main focus is on modelling a users' privacy preferences using privacy profiles. Once a set of privacy profiles is defined, a target user is assigned to the profile that is best matched according to the specific characteristics of that profile. Eventually, based on this assignment, the user is recommended with personalised permission settings. The PPA builds privacy profiles using hierarchical clustering with varied distance measures (Euclidean, Manhattan, Cosine) and with an evaluation of the optimal number of clusters, which appeared to be seven. With regards profiling, the user is asked a set of dynamically generated questions to infer his privacy preferences and, based on the results, is assigned the closest cluster. For the recommendation calculation a SVM classifier has been used so that PPA passes user's features (answers to questions) to the classifier to determine recommendations for privacy settings learned from the training data (seven profiles). Subsequently, PPA displays the list of grouped per permission purpose settings recommendations. Finally, PPA proposes three options of recommendation adaptation that the user can accept: all shown recommendations, selectively accept some recommendations, and reject all recommendations. Actually, this study supports previous research where a common occurring issue in a real-world privacy settings datasets is where a majority of users' privacy settings configuration are set to default values (Gross & Acquisti, 2005; Kaskina, 2018; Liu et al., 2011). Having a prevailing number of default privacy settings in the privacy profile training may affect the model's accuracy. For the sake of the model's accuracy, it is desirable to know the underlying reasons why users tend to use default settings. In addition, not every user can perfectly fit to only one cluster where, most likely, the user can possess characteristics of several profiles (Kaskina, 2018).

4.1.2 Fuzzy-Based Privacy Settings Recommender System (FPRS)

This section introduces the conceptual model for a novel approach of calculating privacy recommendations based on the static privacy profiles. A fuzzy-based privacy recommender system (FPRS) concentrates beyond the multidimensional structure and eliminates discriminative tendencies that appears in traditional classification of privacy profiles by using the results of fuzzy clustering partitioning. Figure 4.1 displays the proposed framework of the system where each component is described in detail below.

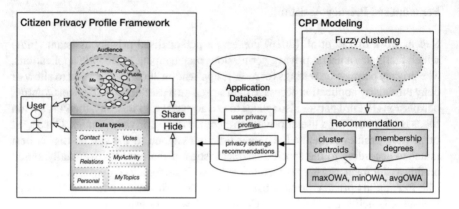

Fig. 4.1 Fuzzy-based privacy recommender system

Citizen Privacy Profile Framework The citizen privacy profile framework described in Sect. 3.1.2 measures a users' actual privacy behaviour on the platform. It contains three objects—the citizen, the data levels and the audience levels; and two possible interactions—the status (share or hide). This framework differs from others by allowing users to set up their visibility preferences to some level of granularity. The implementation of this part is presented in Sect. 2.3.

Database Storage The database stores two different tables. The first stores citizens' current privacy settings that have been derived from the privacy framework, and the second table stores calculated privacy recommendations that will be presented to citizens. The specification of the database storage depends on the scalability of the system. In this work a relational MySQL database is used.

CPP Modelling A distinctive part of this framework is that it introduces the concept of fuzzy privacy profiles for the citizen privacy profile modelling. Fuzzy clustering allows objects to be associated with many clusters according to their membership degree value, based on the fuzzy set theory introduced by Zadeh (1965). It may be an oversimplification problem if relying on a uni- or even multidimensional classification of disclosure behaviours, therefore, this framework suggests considering privacy profiles not only as multidimensional but also as fuzzy. To the best of our knowledge this is a first attempt to interpret the multi-dimensionality and inherent vagueness of user privacy preferences using a fuzzy logic approach. This framework demonstrates to what extent the nuances of citizen privacy behaviours can be captured with the help of fuzzy profile modelling.

Automation Once the citizen privacy profile framework is defined and the set of privacy profiles is modelled, the next step is the automation of the privacy recommendations. For the recommendations calculation a novel approach is proposed and utilises an inferred information from fuzzy clustering results. The implementation of this component is presented in the next section Sect. 4.2. One of the missing parts of the proposed framework is the design of a recommendation presentation to the user. Do we intend to present it as a nudge, or as a list? What action upon the recommendation is the user provided with? Extensive research has been conducted on designing the presentation to the user (Acquisti et al., 2017; Balebako et al., 2011; Wang et al., 2014), however, it is out of scope of this research.

4.2   Implementation of FPRS

4.2.1   Prototype Architecture

Figure 4.2 presents an architecture of the implemented privacy settings recommender system. The architecture consists of two web-servers: Participa Inteligente web-server hosts the CPP framework, MySQL database and user browser display the user interface of the application; ShinyServer web-server hosts the CPP modelling of the conceptual model (see Fig. 4.1) and the application itself is developed in RStudio. The shiny application consists of three R scripts, where the UI.R file runs the user interface of the application, Rec.R file is the server side of the application where the connection to the database and the calculation of the recommendation is performed, Assessment.R script is dedicated to the user evaluation of the system as described in Sect. 4.3.5. All .R scripts main functions are developed using RStudio packages.

4.2.2   Recommendations Calculation

This section presents privacy recommendations calculation based on user privacy profile models as previously described. Before explaining the recommendation algorithm, we recall the advantages of fuzzy clustering. The fuzzy clustering helps

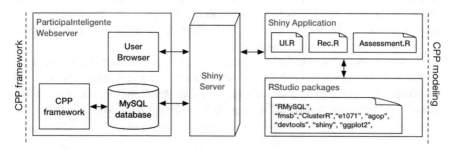

Fig. 4.2 Architecture of fuzzy-based privacy recommender system

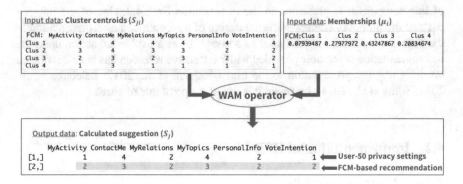

Fig. 4.3 Recommendation for User-50

to define a structure in unclear and undistinctive data by indicating to what degree each observation belongs to every cluster found in the data. Fuzzy clustering can detect differentiated inclination of users' privacy preferences per given data type.

The calculation of privacy recommendations based on fuzzy clustering results is straightforward. We use a set of cluster centroids and the membership degrees for each observation as calculated by fuzzy clustering, and then use weighted average mean (WAM) to aggregate final recommendation values for each dimension (data type). In the prototype,[1] the WAM is calculated using R package "agop".[2] Thus, the recommended privacy setting S_j for a given user, for a particular data level "j", is as follows:

$$S_j = \frac{\sum_{i=1}^{c}(s_{ji} * \mu_i)}{\sum_{i=1}^{c} \mu_i} \tag{4.1}$$

where c is the number of clusters defined as a result of FCM or PAM clustering algorithms; s_{ji} is a privacy setting calculated for each user where j is a particular data level and i is an index of the cluster centroid; μ_i are membership values related to the cluster centroid i. Thus, a cluster's privacy suggestion for a particular user is considered in accordance with his membership degree (weight) belonging to that cluster. In this way, conversely from classic sharp clustering, we consider fuzzy user privacy profile model where opinions of all clusters are integrated in a weighted manner for the final privacy recommendation.

Figure 4.3 shows the calculation example of a privacy recommendation for *User-50* using FCM algorithm with Euclidean distance. For every data type a WAM is calculated according to User-50's membership values to every cluster in the dataset. Thus, the recommendation suggests User-50 open the MyActivity data on

---

[1] https://participacioninteligente.org/survey-privacy.

[2] https://cran.r-project.org/web/packages/agop/agop.pdf.

the platform to friends, while the contactability restricts the public to friends of friends. Also, this algorithm understands that User-50 can open his vote intention from private to friends and restrict the visibility of his political topics from public to friends of friends. The algorithm agrees with the User's-50 initial privacy setting on two data types, MyRelations and PersonalInformation, producing the same visibility values to be opened to friends only. The resulted privacy recommendation appears extremely interesting. Why does the algorithm decide that a user should be more open on her activity and vote intention data, while being more restrictive on her political topics and contactability. Clearly, this outcome is an interplay of the chosen distance metric, the algorithm itself, the way of the initiation of cluster centroids and the existing population of the data. However, the question what will the recommendation be for those data types if the cluster centroids were not initiated as an artificial means in the dataset (case of FCM), however, were taken as some real representatives (case of fuzzy PAM) of the dataset should be raised.

It is sufficiently evident that each clustering algorithm has different behaviours and goals. However, which one works best for the privacy profiles analysis and further recommendation calculation? At this moment it can be clearly identified that, while clustering privacy profiles, two factors should be considered: the initiation of cluster centroids and the distance metric. Although, note not all clustering algorithms uses distance metric. This is a case of the Gustafson–Kessel algorithm which uses a covariance matrix instead of distance metric to detect ellipsoidal forms of clusters, and which has similar results with PAM clustering with Mahalanobis distance. Also, an interesting comparison of recommendation calculation can be made with collaborative filtering (Herlocker et al., 2000). This algorithm is common and widely used in e-Commerce recommender systems. In particular, the comparison can be made with *user-user collaborative filtering*. An intuitive algorithm of this method is that it selects relevant neighbourhoods of user by comparing a target user's profile vector with all user's profiles based on similarity measures like Pearson correlation, cosine or spearman rank correlation. Out of all similarities among users, only the top-N users to a target user are selected, and then the score rating for an item is calculated based on the ratings of the most top similar users weighted by the values of similarity. In our recommendation method, the selected set of the most similar users can be related to our set of cluster centroids. The score for the item (in our case for a data type) is calculated by multiplying centroid scores with the membership degree according to the objective function of the clustering algorithm. In fact, among cluster centroids there is only one most similar centroid, while the rest are representatives of other user models. The property of using opinions from different models (clusters) can possibly superinduce the diversity and serendipity in recommendations. The next section discusses which fuzzy clustering algorithm (FCM or PAM), in combination with different distance metrics, provides the most accurate recommendations.

Table 4.1 Overview of accuracy metrics

Name	Formula	Description
Accuracy	$ACC = \frac{TP+TN}{TP+FP+FN+TN}$	The proportion of elements in actual privacy settings that are equal to the corresponding element in predicted ones
Absolute percent error	$APE = \sum_{i=1}^{n} \frac{|A_i - P_i|}{A_i}$	The element-wise absolute percent difference between actual and predicted privacy settings
Mean absolute error	$MAE = \frac{\sum_{i=1}^{n} |y_i - x_i|}{n}$	The average absolute difference between actual and predicted privacy settings
Mean squared error	$MSE = \frac{1}{n}\sum_{i=1}^{n}(Y_i - \hat{Y}_i)$	The average squared difference between actual and predicted privacy settings
Classification	$CE_i = \frac{f}{n} \times 100$	The proportion of elements in actual privacy settings that are not equal to the corresponding element in predicted

4.2.3 Evaluation of Recommendations Accuracy

In general, the best recommendation is the one that perfectly matches the users' preferences. As we assume that users have already expressed their privacy preferences by defining their privacy settings on their Participa Inteligente accounts on the platform, we investigate the accuracy of calculated recommendations compared to users' initial privacy settings. Thus, the error results between users' actual and recommended privacy settings is compared. If the prediction error is low between actual and recommended settings, this signifies that the privacy recommendation is close to users' preference. If the prediction error is high, then the recommended privacy settings are sufficiently different from users' initial privacy settings. The list of outlined accuracy metrics was calculated using R package "Metrics".[3] These metrics measure the accuracy of provided privacy recommendations when compared with the initial dataset of users' privacy settings (baseline). The baseline was compared with models built upon the following algorithms: fuzzy Partitioning Around Medoids (PAM) clustering with Mahalanobis, Manhattan and Euclidean distances and Fuzzy C-means (FCM) clustering with Manhattan and Euclidean distances (Table 4.1). To avoid overfitting problem, the 10-fold cross validation of each recommender algorithm model was calculated based on validity indexes presented in Table 3.13.

The results displayed in Table 4.2 suggest in the agreement of MAE, MSE, RMSE and CE metrics the best prediction is produced using an FCM algorithm with Euclidean distance of 2 cluster partition. As per the ACC metric the best accuracy of recommendations is achieved with an FCM Euclidean distance of 15 cluster solutions, whereas APE suggest FCM with Manhattan distance with 9 clusters is

---

[3] https://cran.r-project.org/web/packages/Metrics/Metrics.pdf.

Table 4.2 10-fold cross validation of FCM clustering

Metric Algorithm	ACC	APE	MAE	MSE	CE
FCM-Euc-2	**0.42564**	0.50192	0.65897	0.82821	0.57436
FCM-Euc-4	0.51026	0.37692	0.59744	0.81282	0.48974
FCM-Euc-5	0.52564	0.39274	0.60513	0.86667	0.47436
FCM-Euc-7	0.53846	0.34765	0.51282	0.61538	0.46154
FCM-Euc-15	0.69744	0.22179	**0.35128**	**0.44872**	**0.30256**
FCM-Mnh-2	0.53846	0.39637	0.55385	0.73846	0.46154
FCM-Mnh-6	0.56410	0.32265	0.46154	0.51282	0.43590
FCM-Mnh-9	0.69231	**0.19444**	0.43590	0.69231	0.30769
FCM-Mnh-11	0.66667	0.21795	0.43590	0.64103	0.33333
FCM-Mnh-13	0.60256	0.40171	0.58333	1.03205	0.39744
FCM-Mnh-15	0.62393	0.30912	0.43590	0.55556	0.37607

Table 4.3 10-fold cross validation of PAM clustering

Metric Algorithm	ACC	APE	MAE	MSE	CE
PAM-Euc-2	0.38974	0.79530	0.94615	1.61795	0.61026
PAM-Euc-4	0.45385	0.45321	0.66410	0.90000	0.54615
PAM-Euc-15	0.62308	0.28419	0.48974	0.71538	0.37692
PAM-Mnh-2	0.46667	0.45556	0.61538	0.77949	0.53333
PAM-Mnh-3	0.55385	0.38248	0.54615	0.74615	0.44615
PAM-Mnh-5	0.50256	0.38419	0.53077	0.59744	0.49744
PAM-Mnh-6	0.53333	0.34316	0.50000	**0.56667**	0.46667
PAM-Mnh-15	0.63846	**0.26218**	**0.44872**	0.62308	**0.36154**
PAM-Mah-2	**0.34615**	0.83654	1.01795	1.74615	0.65385
PAM-Mah-6	0.50256	0.40000	0.61795	0.85897	0.49744
PAM-Mah-15	0.60769	0.30791	0.51538	0.76154	0.39231

the preferred method. PAM clustering algorithms' results are displayed in Table 4.3. APE, MAE, RMSE and CE metrics show that the best accuracy is performed by PAM Manhattan distance with 15 clusters. The ACC metric indicates the best accuracy using a PAM Mahalanobis distance with 2 clusters, and MSE demonstrates the best predicted privacy settings recommendation using PAM Manhattan with 6 clusters. Moreover, to compare results between the two FCM-based and PAM-based algorithm models, the highest accuracy is performed with the former. The result can be influenced by the fact that, unlike with PAM algorithms where cluster centroids initialised from the dataset, FCM calculates clusters as artificial weighted means which supposedly functions better with a indistinguishable and vague dataset (low dissimilarity). As previously highlighted, there is a low dissimilarity of privacy profiles (Sect. 3.3.1), thereof, the presented clustering models, above, attempt to divide the data into 2 clusters, to separate vectors as granular as possible, so that

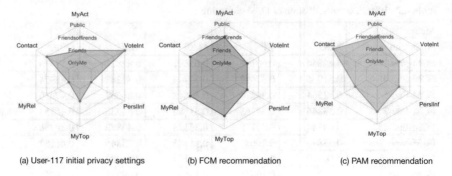

(a) User-117 initial privacy settings   (b) FCM recommendation   (c) PAM recommendation

Fig. 4.4 Recommendation for User-117

vectors can be differentiated. If the recommender system intends to provide highly accurate recommendations that will differ slightly from the users' initial privacy settings, then this solution might be appropriate. However, such partitions do not provide a meaningful classification of the privacy profiles. If the goal is to derive the privacy profile types (personas) existing in the dataset, then FCM with 9 clusters and PAM with 6 cluster would be more relevant but the accuracy will suffer slightly. Moreover, such recommendations can have more diversity or novelty by virtue of its slight inaccuracy. In such a situation, the decision must be taken by the system designer on how to balance the trade-off between accuracy of recommendations and the inference of classification types.

Figure 4.4 demonstrates privacy recommendations produced by models of a FCM-Manhattan-9 and PAM-Manhattan-15 clustering result. User-117 privacy profile is multidimensional, where user prefers to share MyActivity and MyTopics data to friends only. Also, by letting VoteIntention to be open to public, User-117 then prefers to keep PersonalInformation and MyRelations data private. In this case, recommendations generated by both FCM and PAM algorithms suggest to set VoteIntention visible only to friends, and to compensate this decrease of visibility by increasing the visibility of MyActivity and MyTopics to friends of friends visibility, and PersonalInformation to friends instead of being hidden. The FCM-based recommendation suggests if opening the MyRelations data visible to a friends of friends audience then the Contact settings should be closed from public to friends of friends as well. Conversely, PAM-based recommendation considers keeping the Contact visible to public, while sharing MyRelations information only to friends.

An example of User's-79 initial settings (Fig. 4.5) is more open where all data types are visible to the public, except for the MyTopics data which is unshared. For that, both FCM- and PAM-based suggestions agreed on recommending sharing MyActivity, MyTopics and MyRelations to friends of friends and VoteIntention visible to friends only. Both algorithms agree on the contact sharing decision but disagree on privacy decision for the PersonalInfromation data. The FCM-based

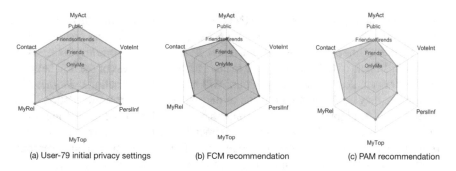

Fig. 4.5 Recommendation for User-79

recommendation regard sharing PersonalInformation data to friends of friends and PAM suggests keeping it visible to friends only.

These examples demonstrate how two algorithms estimate differently on the sharing decision between various data types. In the first example two algorithms were trading the visibility values between Contact and MyRelations data, whereas in the second example, FCM and PAM algorithms produced different opinions for the one data type. In such cases, the question of which algorithm produces a more relevant privacy settings recommendations should be asked. The useful insights can be inferred from user-centric evaluation of the privacy settings recommendations which are presented in the next section.

4.3   User Evaluation of Privacy Recommendations

The analysis of privacy recommendations based on different fuzzy clustering algorithms helped to outline the system aspects that need to be evaluated from the user-centred perspective. There are two foundational frameworks related to the user-centric evaluation of recommender systems. One of them is *ResQue* framework, proposed by Pu et al. (2011) which postulates that perceived recommendation quality, interface adequacy and interaction adequacy has a positive effects on users' beliefs on perceived usefulness, transparency and ease of use of received recommendations. Those beliefs, in turn, have causal effects to their attitudes and, subsequently, increased attitudes would finally affect behavioural intentions, such as intention to return or to recommend the system to friends. However, this model does not allow establishing which specific perception explains the users' experience related to a specific system feature. In addition, it lacks the personalised perception of users towards their experience and attitudes. To solve this problem, a more elaborate evaluation framework model was presented by Knijnenburg et al. (2012). This framework helps to identify in which way the system's critical features (Objective Systems Aspects—OSA) are subjectively perceived by a specific user (Subjective System Aspect—SSA), further investigate how SSA influences user experience

(EXP) and, finally, the interaction (INT) with the system. Thus, this framework helps to identify the effects of OSA on SSA, EXP and INT. The distinguishing part of this framework is that it considers SSA as the opportunity to measure mediating effects of OSA on EXP and to increase the robustness of the link between them. For example, if different algorithms will have high satisfaction outcomes, this experience may be due to a high value of perceived quality recommendation in the case of the first algorithm, while the outcome satisfaction of the second algorithm may be mediated by the perceived recommendation sharpness. In addition, this framework considers other possible moderators of user experience, such as personal characteristics (PC) and situational characteristics (SC). Hence, this framework proposes an ordered and well-structured model, arguing that the user experience is caused by objective system aspects via subjective system aspects and personal or situational characteristics. We will use this framework as blueprint to evaluate privacy recommendations calculated by fuzzy-based privacy settings recommender system.

4.3.1   Objective System Aspects

This section describes which system's features will be evaluated by users and introduces the concepts of *sharp* and *soft* privacy recommendations. *Sharp recommendation* means when the model generates privacy suggestions that are very different from the user's initial privacy settings. These are abrupt recommendations, supposedly, which can evoke strong negative reactions of users. For example, if the user's initial privacy settings tend to have low visibility preferences, such as "visible only to me", a sharp recommendation will suggest opening the data to be visible to "public". Similarly, for the user privacy profile with open privacy preferences, when having visibility settings to "public" the sharp recommendation will suggest to close visibility to "only me". Consequently, sharp recommendations can be subdivided into two types: liberal—over-disclosing ones, and restrictive recommendations—under-disclosing recommendations.

Soft recommendation suggests privacy settings which are very close or almost equal to the user's initial privacy settings. This recommendation provides a gradual change in user's privacy settings. For example, if user's privacy settings tend to have visibility preferences "open only to me" the soft recommendation will gently suggest opening only "to friends", or even in some cases it will recommend keeping the initial privacy setting of the user. In this case, if the user tends to have "public" visibility, the soft recommendation will not abruptly suggest "Hey you are in a danger zone by being public, you better close this data to be private only to yourself". Instead, it will suggest "Your data is visible to all public, would you like making it visible to friends of friends?". The soft recommendation might avoid user reactance, unlike with sharp recommendations.

In Tables 4.2 and 4.3, the highest accuracy was scored by the APE metric with Fuzzy C-means (FCM) Manhattan distance clustering with 9 clusters. This means that the recommendation of privacy settings is very close to users' initial privacy settings. The advantage of this is that the privacy recommendation compromises user's privacy preferences and is more likely to be accepted by the user with a low negative reactance effect. However, if the user's initial privacy settings are a priori known to be inconsistent (affected by privacy paradox), then the model with the highest accuracy will predict erroneous regularities. Therefore, the most accurate algorithm is not necessarily to be the best option. Partitioning Around Medoids (PAM) Manhattan distance clustering with 15 clusters scored the second highest accuracy value, which has a lower prediction accuracy when compared to the FCM algorithm. Then, in this case, the PAM algorithm tends to predict irregularities in the dataset and provides sharper recommendations as they diverge with user's initial privacy preferences. These recommendations might elicit a reactance-style response from users.

Thus, by applying different clustering algorithms, the different types of recommendations can be generated and be further utilised in the system. For example, in the context when a user needs to be given more control over her privacy, or when it is necessary to automate her privacy, the system will be able to provide a relevant recommendation. In our case, soft recommendations favour the user's control, while sharp recommendations tend to automate user's privacy. The user-centric evaluation of this section aims to compare both fuzzy clustering algorithms against the baseline system, which is represented by the users' own privacy settings. Also, the FCM-based recommendations are compared against PAM-based recommendations. To this end, the objective system aspects under investigation are two recommender models—FCM with 9 clusters and PAM with 15 clusters (both using Manhattan distance), and the baseline—users' own privacy settings. To that, the following hypothesises are posed:

- *H.1* Compared to the baseline system, FCM-based recommendations are positively related with perceived recommendation quality, while PAM-based recommendations are negatively related.
- *H.2* Compared to the baseline system, FCM-based recommendations negatively related with the perceived recommendation sharpness, while PAM-based recommendations are positively related.
- *H.3* The perceived recommendation quality is negatively associated with users' reactance experience, while the perceived recommendation sharpness is positively associated with users' reactance.
- *H.4* The perceived recommendation quality is positively associated with users' satisfaction experience, while the perceived recommendation sharpness is negatively associated with users' satisfaction.
- *H.5* The perceived recommendation quality is positively associated with users' persuasion to accept recommendations, while the perceived recommendation sharpness is negatively associated with users' persuasion.
- *H.6* People with consistent privacy behaviour, when presented with soft recommendations, will have the higher perceived recommendation quality and the lower perceived recommendation sharpness, while people with inconsistent

privacy behaviour score low on the perceived quality of the recommendations and high on the perceived recommendation sharpness.

- *H.7* People with consistent privacy behaviour when presented with sharp recommendations will have the lower perceived recommendation quality and the higher perceived recommendation sharpness, while people with inconsistent privacy behaviour score high on the perceived quality of the recommendations and low on the perceived recommendation sharpness.

4.3.2   Subjective System Aspects

Perceived Recommendation Sharpness

Objectively speaking, the accuracy of the recommendation provided by a different algorithm can be quantitatively calculated. However, the level of recommendation accuracy can be perceived differently by a specific user. Therefore, the concepts of sharp and soft recommendations will be evaluated by presenting the concept of the users' *perceived recommendation sharpness (PSH)*. For example, the PSH will be higher when users are presented with the sharp recommendation, and lower when presented with the soft recommendation.

Perceived Recommendation Quality

The initial goal of the recommender system is to finely match the users' interests, preferences or attitudes. The quality of recommendations is one of the determinants of a successful system. The recommender's algorithm performance can be measured by users according to their perceived quality. The perceived quality of recommendation can be associated with various metrics, such as perceived accuracy of the recommendation, ease of use, usefulness, novelty, attractiveness, etc. (Knijnenburg et al., 2011; Pu et al., 2011). Although, the recommendation quality stands close to the recommendation accuracy we do not relate the two as the recommendation accuracy relates much closer to perceived recommendation sharpness. As the perceived recommendation quality can be explained quite broadly, and to avoid the confusion between recommendation's accuracy, sharpness and quality, we will equate perceived recommendation quality with perceived recommendation usefulness. According to Pu et al. (2011), the perceived recommendation usefulness indicates to what extent users find the recommendation being useful, such as how the recommendation improves or facilitates user's decision-making and improves their performance compared to their experience without the recommender system's aid (Pu et al., 2011). Thus, *the perceived recommendation quality (PRQ)* of our system will explain the user's attitudes towards the recommendation efficiency and effectiveness in facilitating a user's privacy decision-making.

4.3.3   User Experience

Persuasion Effect

The recommendation's strength in changing user's attitudes is associated with a *persuasion (PS)* effect in a recommender system. The main source of persuasion is the preference-elicitation-matching process (Gretzel & Fesenmaier, 2006; Tam & Ho, 2005). According to Tam and Ho (2005), a user's willingness to accept a personalised option is higher when the level of preference matching is high, thus, the persuasive effect of the recommendation is higher too. Moreover, persuasion refers to the influence on the user's decision, where the precision of the preference matching is not the only factor for positive persuasion outcome. Kaptein et al. (2012) stated that goals, timing and presentation of the recommendation should be considered as persuasive strategies. For example, Nanou et al. (2010) showed that "structured overview" and "text and video" interfaces are positively correlated with the persuasion effect. In this study, the authors link persuasion effect to the likelihood of selecting recommended options, increase in users' self-efficacy and information quality and sufficiency to lead users to a decision. Cosley et al. (2003) presented the recommendations' tendency to influence users' opinions in case of movie recommender systems. Then, while looking at privacy recommender systems, one might ask "how does privacy recommendation influence user's further privacy attitudes and will it shape his future privacy behaviour?" As Knijnenburg and Jin (2013) mentioned, "recommender system should carefully consider the privacy sharing options, because it can influence users to share significantly more without a substantial difference in comfort". Taking into consideration the possible influence and persuasion power of recommendations over user's final privacy decision, the recommender privacy system should carefully consider the algorithm in selecting between a sharp or soft recommendation type. The virtue of the recommendation concept already entails a positive perception of the recommended item, if user experienced is a satisfactory interaction with the recommender (Cremonesi et al., 2012). The perceived quality of recommendation is an indirect indicator of the potential recommendation's persuasion effect (Cremonesi et al., 2012). Therefore, if the quality of the recommendation is satisfying, then the persuasion effect of the privacy recommendation will be higher. In our framework, soft recommendations are more accurate than sharp ones.

Reactance Effect

A reactance effect upon recommendation options has been scarcely investigated in the field of recommender systems. A reactance is a user's negative behaviour evoked through experiencing a recommended option. If the user feels a threat to his freedom of choice, then the reactance behaviour can be developed towards the recommendation advice (Aljukhadar et al., 2017). Fitzsimons and Lehmann (2004) suggests that if the recommendation does not meet the user's initial expectations about choice options, then he will ignore and act against this recommendation, thus, expressing his reactance behaviour. Other factors such as perceived expertise level of the recommendation source, situational context and personal characteristics play a role upon the elicited reactance state of the user. Aljukhadar et al. (2017) discovered that the reactance behaviour alters the level of trust in a recommendation. However, the trust effect is, in turn, mediated by the person's self-construal state. People who look for similarity with others, and have a high need to socialise and conform to others, are considered to be with an interdependent self-construal state. While users with an independent self-construal state will be less affected by the trust in others and, contrarily, they will rely on their own objective evaluation of the item rather than on the trustworthiness of the recommender system. Therefore, people with an activated interdependent self-state tend to have a higher trust in the provided recommendation and, thus, are more likely to have less reactance behaviour. In contrast, people with activated independent self-construal have higher reactance, as they have a lower trust in recommendations. Thus, three intrinsic characteristics of reactance can be delineated: recommendation's fit to user's initial expectation, recommender trustworthiness and user's self-construal state. The reactance may most probably appear with privacy recommendations as privacy has more sensitive context than, for example, e-commerce recommendations. As sharp recommendations are more inconsistent with a user's initial expectations, it is assumed that the sharp recommendation will evoke a user's higher reactance behaviour than soft recommendations.

Outcome Satisfaction

Outcome satisfaction is the one of main measures of a users' experience with a recommender system. Different factors influence user's satisfaction, and it is the most commonly related to perceived recommendation quality (Bharati & Chaudhury, 2004; Knijnenburg et al., 2011; Pu et al., 2011). Therefore, the subjective system aspects of our framework, such as the perceived recommendation quality, might have an effect on the user's recommendation's satisfaction. In addition, it is assumed that the perceived recommendation sharpness is associated with the perceived recommendation quality, thereof the overall satisfaction may also depend on the recommendation sharpness.

4.3.4   Personal Characteristics

Inconsistent/Consistent Privacy Behaviour

Having sharp or soft recommendation types might solve other factors, such as *consistent/inconsistent privacy behaviour* which was addressed in the previous evaluation in Sect. 3.4.4. As an example, for people with consistent privacy behaviour, where user's privacy attitude aligns with the actual privacy behaviour, the system should be very cautious with regards privacy recommendations, thus, it would be better to provide soft recommendations. In contrast, for people with an inconsistent privacy behaviour, the sharp recommendation can be an appropriate solution. As an example, in case when the user's profile is public, restrictive recommendation can support them to suggest more restrictive settings.

4.3.5   Evaluation Setup

Experimental Manipulations

The aim of the user experiment is to compare privacy settings recommendations generated by different fuzzy clustering algorithms (FCM with 9 clusters and PAM with 15 clusters based on Manhattan distance) and users' own privacy settings. The clustering-based recommender system is compared against a non-personalised system, which is represented by the users' own privacy settings (*baseline of the system*). As the recommender system cannot always reassure the superiority over the non-personalised system, the condition of comparing it with the proposed baseline becomes relevant (Knijnenburg & Willemsen, 2015). The two objective systems aspects (FCM- and PAM-based recommendations) are manipulated in the single experiment, leading to the *simultaneous within-subjects* experiment with 2 experimental conditions. Such manipulation allows users to compare the different algorithms and choose the best one they like, including the baseline proposition (Knijnenburg & Willemsen, 2015). The advantage of this experiment setting is that subtle differences between conditions can be detected, which is highly relevant for the case of this research. The disadvantage of such experimental settings is that it lacks the realistic presentation of the system, however, by presenting all options at the same time decreases the feeling of the experiment.

Experimental Procedures

The participants were recruited via online email invitation (see Sect. C.1, Fig. C.1) addressed to the users of the Participa Inteligente platform. The same set of users who participated in the first evaluation study (Sect. 3.4.4) were invited. In the email invitation, participants are directed to the website of the user evaluation application.[4] The invitation email, the instructions and exercises areas, as well as the survey questionnaire, were translated into the Spanish language by Prof. Dr. Luis Teran who is a native Spanish speaker. The user evaluation application includes *the*

---

[4] https://participacioninteligente.org/survey-privacy.

instructions area (see Sect. C.1, Fig. C.2) which explains how to proceed with the application and *the exercise area* (see Sect. C.1, Fig. C.3), where the privacy settings recommendations are presented to the user with the follow-up survey questionnaire (see Sect. C.1, Table B.2). The first 100 users who completed the survey received a reward for their participation, a book titled *"eDemocracy & eGovernment. Etapas hacia la sociedad democratica del Conocimiento, por A.Meier y L. Teran"*.

Once the user logged into the exercise area, they were provided with the short exercise instructions followed by privacy settings recommendations as displayed in Fig. C.3. As this is a within-subject evaluation, there are three privacy recommendation options presented to the user: "option 1" displays the user's own initial privacy settings; "option 2"—recommendation generated by the PAM algorithm with 15 clusters based on Manhattan distance; "option 3"—recommendation generated by the FCM algorithm with 9 clusters based on Manhattan distance. The initial user's privacy settings are intentionally presented as the recommendation option in order to have a comparison with a baseline, and also to distinguish those users who expressed "privacy paradox" behaviour. As such, if the user chose a privacy recommendation of their own privacy settings values, it means that the user performs consistent privacy behaviour. At this step, users are asked to select one privacy recommendation option that they prefer and are then invited to start a survey within the application. In the next sections, the details of the construct measurement development are described.

Defining Measurements

According to Knijnenburg and Willemsen (2015), while developing the construct it should maintain the content validity. This means that each construct must consist of at least three items to preserve its conceptual nature. It is also suggested to refer to the existing literature when selecting the measurement scale for a specific construct. However, when introducing the new construct which does not appear in the existing literature, its content validity should be carefully considered and be represented with at least with five items. According to the evaluation framework displayed in Fig. 4.6, the following constructs addressed for the evaluation (see Sect. C.1, Table B.2): *privacy behaviour consistency (PBC), perceived sharpness (PSH), perceived quality (PRQ), outcome satisfaction (OS), reactance (RC) and persuasion (PS)*. Thus, the questions for *the perceived quality* have been adapted from Knijnenburg et al. (2012) and Pu et al. (2011), *the persuasion* were partially adapted from Nanou et al. (2010), *the reactance* have been partially adapted from Hennig-Thurau et al. (2012). *The perceived sharpness* is a new concept presented for the evaluation of the recommendation, therefore, related questions were discussed with an expert and reduced to five items. The Likert scale *(totally disagree; disagree; neutral; agree; totally agree)* was used for the answer categories of the questions.

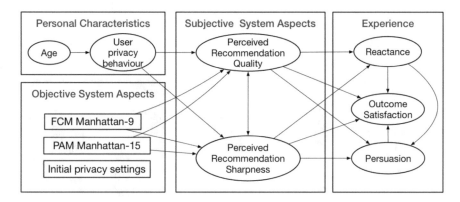

Fig. 4.6 Privacy recommendation evaluation framework

4.3.6   Evaluation Analysis

The user evaluation commenced on November 13th, 2017 and ended on January 31st, 2018. The dataset of collected responses consists of 20 participants' answers. Among them 17 males and 3 females aged between 21 and 67 years old (median age is 37.5). Unfortunately, the larger number of participants was not achieved which poses doubt on the robustness of the statistical analysis based on this dataset. Therefore, it will be not possible to establish the validity of the proposed constructs with a small dataset. Admitting the fact that the data does not attain the statistical significance, the aforementioned hypothesises will not be approved or rejected. Among the participant's answers for the chosen privacy recommendation, 14 users out 20 (70%) chose the first option—which represents user's initial privacy settings of her profile, whereas 3 users (15%) preferred to choose privacy settings suggested by PAM-based algorithm, and the other 3 users (15%) accepted the recommendation generated by FCM-based algorithm. Figure 4.7 displays the preliminary results of the collected data.

Perceived quality—on average, users with own and FCM-based privacy settings recommendations score higher on the perceived quality compared to users with PAM-based recommendations.

Perceived sharpness—the lower the sharpness, the higher is the mismatch of the provided privacy settings recommendations. On average, users perceived higher mismatch with PAM-based recommendations. Among the users who chose own privacy settings, 42.8% agreed that the privacy options mismatch with their privacy preferences and 57.1% disagree that recommended privacy options are similar to their privacy attitudes. Such opinions may indicate users' inconsistent privacy behaviour—by stating that the chosen privacy settings do not match their privacy attitudes, in fact they have chosen their own privacy settings. This is an example of the paradoxical privacy behaviour, where users attitudes diverge with their actual

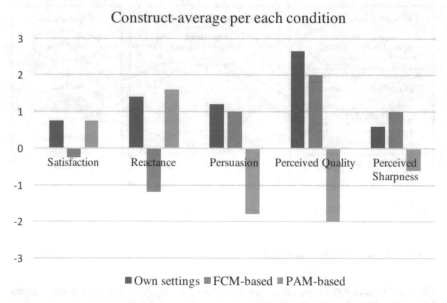

Fig. 4.7 Results of each construct per each privacy settings recommendation condition

privacy preferences. This statement is not statistically justified but showcases the existence of such behaviour.

Outcome satisfaction—on average, users were equally satisfied with their own privacy settings and PAM-based privacy settings recommendation. Amongst users who chose their own privacy settings, 49.9% of them agree that those recommendations were a waste of the time. It may signify that these users were not entirely satisfied with provided recommendations (own privacy settings). However, it is important to encounter that users' own privacy settings were framed as "the recommendation provided by the system"; therefore, such results can be biased by the framing effect. Users who chose FCM-based privacy settings recommendations are less satisfied compared to other two options.

Reactance—on average, users experienced less reactance with FCM-based recommendations, and the highest reactance was with PAM-based recommendations. Among users who chose their own privacy settings, 28.6% expressed to be angry with the limited freedom while presented with recommended privacy settings and they felt frustrated in their attempts to make an independent decision. This may indicate that the majority of participants who chose own privacy settings still experienced the reactance effect upon receiving this recommendation.

Persuasion—on average, users are highly persuaded with their own privacy settings, whereas the PAM-based recommendations have the lowest persuasion effect. The FCM-based recommendations has slightly lower persuasion compared to own settings, but higher than PAM-based recommendation. Interesting to note that

FCM-based recommendation has the lower reactance effect, and a higher persuasion effect.

There should be considered several significant limitations of this user study. The first limitation is the definition of the constructs with its questionnaire items. The constructs of the perceived quality and the perceived sharpness in essence define the accuracy of the provided recommendations. However, this study refers the quality to the perceived usefulness and the sharpness to the perceived accuracy of the recommendations. To highlight the difference between these constructs, Fig. 4.7 displays that own privacy settings are considered more useful (higher perceived quality) but less accurate (lower perceived sharpness) compared to algorithm-calculated recommendations. Another example, even with a high score on the perceived quality and sharpness and consequently less reactance effect, users with FCM-based recommendations still scored low on its satisfaction. The second limitation is the collected number of user responses, which did not allow to derive statistically significant conclusions. It did not permit to conduct a reasonable CFA analysis to investigate the discriminant and convergent validity of the proposed constructs. Moreover, the low N of participation did not allow conducting the robust analysis of the baseline (own privacy settings option) against algorithm-calculated recommendations (14 with own privacy settings versus 6 with algorithm-based recommendations). The third limitation is that the participants' experimental condition was self-selected presented with three options: users' own privacy settings framed as a recommendation, FCM-based and PAM-based privacy settings recommendations. The entire set of participants were presented with the same list with no randomisation of the choices order, thus the results was also affected by the ordering effect. Therefore, this study lacked the counterbalancing procedure. The forth limitation is the users' understanding of the presented visu-alisation of privacy settings recommendations. Not every user can understand and interpret the presented visualisation of privacy settings; therefore, the chosen option can be biased, for example by the anchor effect. To avoid the understanding issues, the users could be explained how to interpret the radar charts, so that they could have been accustomed to the use of such graphs.

This is a first user-centric evaluation framework specifically designed for the privacy settings recommendations. Its limitations are described above, but the possible improvements should be considered for the future work. In future, the clear goal of the user evaluation should be defined. Does the evaluation compare the baseline system against the one of the algorithm-based recommendation (own privacy settings versus FCM-based recommendation)? Or the evaluation aims to compare user experience between two proposed systems (FCM-based versus PAM-based recommendations)? The clear evaluation goal will then advise the design of the experiment. If the baseline system to be compared with one of the algorithm-calculated privacy setting recommendation, then a within-subject experiment could be conducted. For that, a total size of 31 participants (based on G power analysis) can produce statistically significant results. To introduce the counterbalancing effect half of the sample size can be presented with the first choice of the baseline system, whereas the other half of participants with the algorithm-based system as the first option. To evaluate the difference between FCM and PAM systems, the between-subject evaluation can be also designed. For that, a total size of 59 participants (based on G power analysis) will be required, where each half of participants should be randomly assigned to each condition either to FCM or to PAM recommendations.

4.4   Conclusions

The insights derived from the user-centric evaluation concluded that different people will perceive the proposed privacy recommendations differently. All three conditions (users' own privacy settings, FCM-based privacy settings, and PAM-based privacy settings) were presented as "the recommendations calculated by the system". The subjective system aspects like the perceived quality and sharpness of the recommendations scored high on its usefulness and accuracy with the baseline and FCM-based recommendation. The expressed user experience differs among participants' too. Users who chose baseline and FCM-based recommendations had experienced less reactance towards the recommendations, rather than users who chose PAM-based system. Moreover, the clear distinction can be observed between PAM-based and FCM-based privacy settings. Users perceived FCM-based recommendations softer (higher perceived sharpness) and more useful (higher perceived quality), whereas PAM-based recommendation attained users' higher outcome satisfaction, but simultaneously a higher reactance state.

References

Acquisti, A., Adjerid, I., Balebako, R., Brandimarte, L., Cranor, L. F., Komanduri, S., Leon, P. G., Sadeh, N., Schaub, F., Sleeper, M., et al. (2017). Nudges for privacy and security: Understanding and assisting users? Choices online. *ACM Computing Surveys (CSUR), 50*(3), 44.

Aljukhadar, M., Trifts, V., & Senecal, S. (2017). Consumer self-construal and trust as determinants of the reactance to a recommender advice. *Psychology & Marketing, 34*(7), 708–719.

Bahirat, P., He, Y., Menon, A., & Knijnenburg, B. (2018). A data-driven approach to developing IoT privacy-setting interfaces. In *23rd International Conference on Intelligent User Interfaces* (pp. 165–176). ACM.

Balebako, R., Leon, P. G., Almuhimedi, H., Kelley, P. G., Mugan, J., Acquisti, A., Cranor, L. F., & Sadeh, N. (2011). Nudging users towards privacy on mobile devices. In *Proc. CHI 2011 Workshop on Persuasion, Nudge, Influence and Coercion.*

Bharati, P., & Chaudhury, A. (2004). An empirical investigation of decision-making satisfaction in web-based decision support systems. *Decision Support Systems, 37*(2), 187–197.

Cosley, D., Lam, S. K., Albert, I., Konstan, J. A., & Riedl, J. (2003). Is seeing believing? how recommender system interfaces affect users' opinions. In *Proceedings of the SIGCHI Conference on Human Factors in Computing Systems* (pp. 585–592). ACM.

Cremonesi, P., Garzotto, F., & Turrin, R. (2012). Investigating the persuasion potential of recommender systems from a quality perspective: An empirical study. *ACM Transactions on Interactive Intelligent Systems (TiiS), 2*(2), 11.

Dong, C., Jin, H., & Knijnenburg, B. P. (2016). PPM: A privacy prediction model for online social networks. In *International Conference on Social Informatics* (pp. 400–420). Springer.

Fang, L., & LeFevre, K. (2010). Privacy wizards for social networking sites. In *Proceedings of the 19th International Conference on World Wide Web*.

Fitzsimons, G. J., & Lehmann, D. R. (2004). Reactance to recommendations: When unsolicited advice yields contrary responses. *Marketing Science, 23*(1), 82–94.

Ghazinour, K., Matwin, S., & Sokolova, M. (2013). Yourprivacyprotector: A recommender system for privacy settings in social networks. *International Journal of Security, Privacy and Trust Management, 2*(4).

Gretzel, U., & Fesenmaier, D. R. (2006). Persuasion in recommender systems. *International Journal of Electronic Commerce, 11*(2), 81–100.

Gross, R., & Acquisti, A. (2005). Information revelation and privacy in online social networks. In *Proceedings of the 2005 ACM Workshop on Privacy in the Electronic Society* (pp. 71–80).

Hennig-Thurau, T., Marchand, A., & Marx, P. (2012). Can automated group recommender systems help consumers make better choices? *Journal of Marketing, 76*(5), 89–109.

Herlocker, J. L., Konstan, J. A., & Riedl, J. (2000). Explaining collaborative filtering recommendations. In *Proceedings of the 2000 ACM Conference on Computer Supported Cooperative Work* (pp. 241–250). ACM.

Kaptein, M., De Ruyter, B., Markopoulos, P., & Aarts, E. (2012). Adaptive persuasive systems: a study of tailored persuasive text messages to reduce snacking. *ACM Transactions on Interactive Intelligent Systems (TiiS), 2*(2), 10.

Kaskina, A. (2018). Exploring nuances of user privacy preferences on a platform for political participation. In *2018 International Conference on eDemocracy & eGovernment (ICEDEG)* (pp. 89–94). IEEE.

Knijnenburg, B. P., & Jin, H. (2013). The persuasive effect of privacy recommendations. In *Twelfth Annual Workshop on HCI Research in MIS*.

Knijnenburg, B. P., & Willemsen, M. C. (2015). Evaluating recommender systems with user experiments. In *Recommender Systems Handbook* (pp. 309–352). Springer.

Knijnenburg, B. P., Willemsen, M. C., Gantner, Z., Soncu, H., & Newell, C. (2012). Explaining the user experience of recommender systems. *User Modeling and User-Adapted Interaction, 22*(4–5), 441–504.

Knijnenburg, B. P., Willemsen, M. C., & Kobsa, A. (2011). A pragmatic procedure to support the user-centric evaluation of recommender systems. In *Proceedings of the Fifth ACM Conference on Recommender Systems* (pp. 321–324). ACM.

Liu, B., Andersen, M. S., Schaub, F., Almuhimedi, H., Zhang, S., Sadeh, N., Acquisti, A., & Agarwal, Y. (2016). Follow my recommendations: A personalized privacy assistant for mobile app permissions. In *Symposium on Usable Privacy and Security*.

Liu, Y., Gummadi, K., Krishnamurthy, B., & Mislove, A. (2011). Analyzing Facebook privacy settings: user expectations vs. reality. In *Proceedings of the 2011 ACM SIGCOMM Conference on Internet Measurement Conference* (pp. 61–70).

Munemasa, T., & Iwaihara, M. (2011). Trend analysis and recommendation of users? Privacy settings on social networking services. In *International Conference on Social Informatics*, (pp. 184–197). Springer.

Naini, K. D., Altingovde, I. S., Kawase, R., Herder, E., & Niederée, C. (2015). Analyzing and predicting privacy settings in the social web. In *International Conference on User Modeling, Adaptation, and Personalization* (pp. 104–117). Springer.

Nanou, T., Lekakos, G., & Fouskas, K. (2010). The effects of recommendations? Presentation on persuasion and satisfaction in a movie recommender system. *Multimedia Systems, 16*(4–5), 219–230.

Pu, P., Chen, L., & Hu, R. (2011). A user-centric evaluation framework for recommender systems. In *Proceedings of the Fifth ACM Conference on Recommender Systems* (pp. 157–164). ACM.

Tam, K. Y., & Ho, S. Y. (2005). Web personalization as a persuasion strategy: An elaboration likelihood model perspective. *Information Systems Research, 16*(3), 271–291.

Wang, Y., Leon, P. G., Acquisti, A., Cranor, L. F., Forget, A., & Sadeh, N. (2014). A field trial of privacy nudges for Facebook. In *Proceedings of the 32nd Annual ACM Conference on Human Factors in Computing Systems* (pp. 2367–2376). ACM.
Westin, A. F. (1968). Privacy and freedom. *Washington and Lee Law Review, 25*(1), 166.
Zadeh, L. (1965). Fuzzy sets. *Information and Control, 8*(3), 338–353.

Chapter 5
Conclusions

5.1 Discussions

5.1.1 Implication to the Public Need

This research focused on a problem of citizen's privacy behaviour on the platform for political participation called Participa Inteligente. Participa Inteligente (PI) platform is an academic project that arises from the concern for citizen misinformation on policy statements and allows citizens to generate spaces for discussion and participation in topics of interest to the society. This platform aims to enhance civic participation and empowerment by providing different types of recommendations (political topics, groups, articles and users, among others) according to the citizens' needs. This platform expects to facilitate citizens' decision-making by giving them more information and resources to debate. However, the extent to which citizens' willingness to actively participate on the platform by disclosing political interests or opinions depends on the personal desire of disclosure.

Accessible regulation of one's boundaries of private spheres with respect to her interaction and content sharing with others may influence citizen's participation on the platform. This research provided a functional space where users are able to express their desired level of privacy by explicitly defining privacy settings of their accounts. Specifically, the designed citizen privacy profile framework determined essential components for building a privacy management tool for an online platform, where the framework's components were customised and implemented to the needs of PI platform and its context. The consequent study has investigated the use of privacy management tool by citizens from Ecuador which has showed that the majority of users who created accounts on the platform let their privacy settings to be public by default. These results readdress the issue of privacy paradox demonstrating that, indeed, users' actual decisions of being private in most cases diverge with their initial privacy intentions.

A. Kaskina, *Citizen Privacy Framework*, Fuzzy Management Methods,
https://doi.org/10.1007/978-3-031-06021-2_5

This thesis entangles information system technologies such as recommender systems, voting advice applications and privacy by design. Among few privacy recommender systems, this thesis proposes the conceptual design of a fuzzy-based privacy settings recommender system, which applies model-based approach using a real-world dataset of users' privacy settings. The system was implemented on PI platform, which is a case of a voting advice application. In the context of the voting advice applications, the integration of fuzzy-based recommender system can subsequently not only preserve citizens' privacy on an automatic basis but also facilitate their participation on political matters by releasing their cognition load from the burden of privacy decision-making. In general, the development of fuzzy-based privacy settings recommender system involved a full cycle of the privacy by design approach. Initially, the system was entirely designed to the needs of the voting advice application, considering the data types generated, available functionality of privacy management tool, and user population engaged, prior to the development and launch into the production of the platform itself.

The two artefacts—the citizen privacy profile framework and the prototype of the fuzzy-based privacy settings recommender system can be adapted by various organisations. It can be useful functionality for governmental institutions, NGOs, or private online service providers, and be applied to various cases and situational contexts, as the components represent the foundational parts of one's privacy settings configuration in online space. The utmost utility of both artefacts was focused on users of the platform, such that by analysing their privacy behaviour to provide an optimised solution to their privacy settings configurations. Thus, the central part of the provided solution are the citizens, however, the optimisation goals might differ depending on the context of the platform. As an example, the system may not fully automate users' privacy decision-making, but instead, to determine a reasonable balance between automation and user's manual control.

5.1.2 Implication to the Knowledge Base

A profound critical analysis of a privacy-related body of research was conducted (Bélanger & Crossler, 2011; Netter et al., 2013; Smith et al., 2011). It revealed that the majority of studies lacked the design and action research towards actual implementation (Bélanger & Crossler, 2011). In addition, it is recommended to utilise a broader diversity of sample populations, such as avoiding using only student populations, or focusing only on U.S. centric population. The research presented in this thesis fulfils the outlined critics. First, this thesis focused on designing an IT artefact based on the conceptual framework presented then with a practical solution (prototype). Second, the empirical study is based on a diverse population which is not limited to the age, gender, occupation (non-student involved) and focused on Ecuadorian citizens. Third, the analysis of user privacy behaviour was conducted in the contextual scope of the political participation.

The introduced notion of fuzzy privacy profiles not only extends the knowledge base of privacy domain but also proposes a novel approach of quantifying user privacy behaviour. By stipulating the multifaceted nature of each individual, fuzzy privacy profiles encompass all-inclusive underlying patterns of privacy behaviour in the given dataset. It is a next step further from multidimensionality to fuzziness of people's privacy behaviour. Indeed, fuzziness deals with vagueness, uncertainty and imprecision which are inherent characteristics of privacy decision-making. As John et al. (2010) mentioned, information disclosure is seen as a decision problem, in which the decision-maker has to trade-off several uncertain consequences. Moreover, when individuals are uncertain of their preferences their decisions can be influenced by contextual cues or cognitive heuristics.

As stated by Von Alan et al. (2004), the design science research addresses what are considered to be wicked problems. The wicked problem addressed in this thesis is highly related to "a critical dependence upon human cognitive abilities to produce effective solutions". The paradoxical nature of people's privacy behaviours can be justified due to a complexity of people's privacy perceptions within online environments. Therefore, as shown in Chap. 2, people more often refer to cognitive abilities in solving privacy-related issues, as opposed to relying on the rational decisions. Moreover, when dealing with classification of privacy types, people usually find it difficult associating themselves with a given label or class as their attitudes, preferences and decision-making are vague and uncertain by its nature. In such case, applying fuzzy logic facilitates in dealing with humans' perceptions and cognitive estimations, thus, providing more accurate and personalised solutions. The application of fuzzy-based techniques to analyse user privacy behaviour and the introduction of fuzzy privacy profiles is the first attempt done by this work. Moreover, no previous studies focused on the user-centric evaluation of privacy settings recommendations. In addition, the dataset used for the fuzzy clustering techniques represents a real-world data collected from PI platform. Compared to previous studies, non-traditional machine learning methodologies were applied such as Fuzzy C-means and Partitioning Around Medoids clustering algorithms.

5.1.3 Limitations of the Research

During this thesis, several issues were encountered that limited the results of the research. The amount of the collected dataset of user privacy settings was comparatively small—it was possible to retrieve only 391 valid user privacy profiles. Among observations, the majority of profiles were users with default privacy settings. This reflects people's behaviour in a real-world environment, however, it was more challenging to detect patterns while clustering the dataset as the biggest cluster of users with default privacy settings affected the classification of other users, which only slightly differ from the majority.

Privacy profiles, where users' privacy decisions are the same across all data types, can be downgraded into a unidimensional representation. This is also relevant to the case of users with default privacy settings as their all data types are visible to public. The issue confronted with unidimensional profiles is that the proposed fuzzy-based privacy settings recommender system fails to calculate a multidimensional privacy settings recommendation for such profiles. Thus, the recommender system is valid only for the multidimensional privacy profiles.

While proposing an alternative clustering techniques over a traditional sharp clustering approaches, this thesis withdraws a detailed comparison of both, fuzzy and sharp clustering algorithms. An absent comparison of approaches limits to scientifically state if the proposed fuzzy methodologies are indeed outperformed the traditional clustering techniques, thus creating a space for future research to be done in this direction.

During user-centric evaluations, unfortunately, a sufficient amount of the data from both evaluations—user privacy behaviour and privacy settings recommendations—was not collected which did not allow to present statistically signification inferences (only some conclusions could be derived). Additionally, the entire research is restricted to the context of users engaged in the platform for political participation, where the cultural background of the users is monogamous, thus, the conclusions from the user-centric evaluations could not be generalised.

5.1.4 Answering Research Questions

This thesis addressed the existing issues of user privacy behaviour by developing two artefacts in the context of political participation: the citizen privacy profile framework and fuzzy-based privacy settings recommender system (Fig. 5.1). The research questions posed in the beginning of the thesis (Sect. 1.3) are answered below:

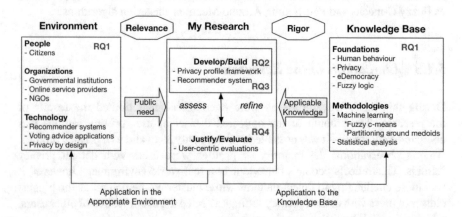

Fig. 5.1 Adapted framework of the Ph.D. with research questions

RQ1. How can a user privacy profile be designed on a platform for political participation? The citizen privacy profile framework was designed and developed based on the extensive literature review. In particular, the components of the framework constitute the general privacy decision-making process: the owner of the data (User) who possesses her own data (Data levels) and interacts with her social network (Audience levels) on the platform. At the moment of information disclosure the user defines her sharing decision by assigning the status of "share" or "hide" to a particular data level visible to a chosen audience level. Such framework defines a simple privacy decision-making process which can be applied to various applications besides the platforms with the context of political participation. The framework does not account dynamic parameters of privacy decision-making process (e.g., keeping track of the change over time), therefore, the privacy profiles on this platform are static.

RQ2. How do fuzzy clustering techniques unveil users' disclosure behaviour on a political platform? The research results demonstrated that a majority of user privacy profiles are multidimensional, if not unidimensional, but undistinguishable and differentiate slightly from other users on particular dimensions. As a result, it becomes difficult to model user privacy profiles with traditional sharp approaches as the algorithm should be capable to detect slight differences. In this case, fuzzy clustering techniques help to differentiate among hardly distinguishable users. Fuzzy clustering unveiled that multidimensional profiles inherently have fuzzy nature, where one user can simultaneously belong to several privacy profiles. By quantifying user privacy behaviour as fuzzy profiles, the hidden information on data structure can be retrieved which, in turn, improves the accuracy and personalisation of privacy settings recommendations.

RQ3. How can an architecture for a fuzzy-based recommender system for privacy settings be designed? The fuzzy-based privacy settings recommender system concept was designed and implemented based on the client-server architecture. Primarily, the parts of the recommender system constitute the components inferred from the fuzzy privacy profiles modelling. The accuracy evaluation of generated recommendations indicated which clustering models provide the most accurate recommendations. The proposed architecture does not solve the questions of scalability and performance efficiency. The essential goal of the system was to present a novel approach of the fuzzy privacy profiles modelling and the calculation of privacy settings recommendation. Preliminary results of the user-centric evaluation demonstrated that on average the fuzzy clustering-based privacy settings recommendation has the potential to be adopted by users as it had a lower reactance effect from users when compared to the baseline system. Also, the evaluation results illustrated that the user preference was expressed for the FCM-based recommendations rather than the PAM-based ones.

RQ4. What are the advantages and disadvantages of applying fuzzy-based approaches in user privacy decision-making? The scarcity of the data is the biggest disadvantage for applying machine learning techniques. Indeed, the dataset of users' privacy profiles is hard to obtain. This research argues that the fuzzy clustering approach facilitates to precisely quantify the privacy profile models even with a comparatively small amount of data. One might have a question why the dimensionality reduction technique was not used. This would be relevant when dimensionality reduction techniques (e.g., PCA, Sammon mapping) are needed to improve visualisation of the data by reducing less variant dimensions. However, the disadvantage of this is that sufficient information can be missed. In contrast, the goal of this thesis was not to provide a proper visualisation of the dataset, but to respect the hidden characteristics of every dimension, as the privacy data is already scarce. Another advantage of fuzzy-based approach over a non-fuzzy one is that it deals better with an identification of the overlapped cluster structures. This research reported that fuzzy-based modelling suggests the fine-grained partitioning (15 clusters) as well as medium (6 or 9 clusters). A fine-grained solution might be irrelevant when determining the classification labels (e.g., for defining privacy persona types), then, in this case, a medium partitioning can be used while at the same time maintaining information to what degree people belong to each partition type.

In some situations, privacy automation can go against the user empowerment. Automation can hold certain risks in terms of its validity and/or ensuing consequences in case of a recommendation adoption. If the user's actual privacy behaviour is deviant from his privacy attitudes, then a system model based on this fallacious data can be considered as unreliable. In this situation, a fuzzy-based approach has a disadvantage as the models built upon the proposed privacy framework are static. Static models have a higher risk to overlook the attitude–behaviour gap issue (privacy paradox). To improve privacy models, dynamic cues, such as psychological or sociological aspects of users, must be considered. Another potential risk is that the algorithm can "unintentionally" shape the user's privacy behaviour, which relates to the filter bubble issue (Knijnenburg et al., 2016) and/or persuasion effect (Cremonesi et al., 2012) of recommendations. However, by categorising recommendations into sharp or soft types, as it was proposed in this thesis, it can help to alleviate such problem by balancing the trade-off between automation and the users' manual control.

5.2   Future Outlook

People's privacy behaviour can be faced with uncertainty upon rational privacy decision as it frequently comes along with overtaxing calculation between the benefits and risks. It becomes challenging to find an optimal solution between the level of privacy support automation and the delegation of a privacy control to its direct owners (users). To reassure the success of such systems intending to support users' privacy in online platforms, the following areas need to be addressed for future research:

Modelling of User Privacy Profiles The modelling of user profiles should go beyond the rational approaches and multidimensional structure. The first undertaken step was presented by this thesis, proposing a novel quantification of privacy profiles, by introducing fuzzy privacy profiles. However, relying solely on the fuzzy profiling is insufficient. Among the contextualisation parameters, variables such as time, trust and emotion-driven attitudes should be addressed in more detail. In particular, the emotion-driven user privacy profiling can give useful insights to the relevance of the privacy recommendations, as well as the recommendation's interface design (e.g., nudge, lists, etc.). Emotions are heavily involved in human's decision-making processes. As Glimcher and Rustichini (2004) stated "Emotion would play an important role in decision-making not just for the worst as was then traditional view but for the better. The emotional malfunction altered the cognitive process. "Emotional" decision-making operates non-consciously, but quite effectively on parameters of *reward, punishment and risk*". Indeed, the highlighted parameters of reward and risk are essential parts in the privacy decision-making.

The Users' Perceptions Towards Privacy Recommendations   This topic should be carefully addressed by researchers. Being on the secondary position the role of privacy settings, especially of privacy recommendations, is often overlooked. While shopping online the recommender system that provides products recommendation may be positively perceived by users as it helps them to accomplish their initial task. However, while using social networking sites for the communication with friends, or for professional networking, receiving privacy recommendations while interacting with the platform may become disturbing and annoying. As the privacy settings recommendations are not broadly exploited, like the recommendations of products, people, etc., the analysis of users' perceptions towards receiving privacy recommendations can provide additional information for the design of privacy recommender systems. This thesis made the first attempt to analyse the users' perception towards privacy recommendations via the persuasion and reactance effect, which needs to be developed in greater detail.

Techniques for Calculating Privacy Recommendations   The modelling of the user privacy profiles plays an important role in building privacy settings recommender system. The future work can also focus on the accuracy of the fuzzy privacy profiles by tweaking the parameters of the fuzzy clustering algorithms. This research has investigated only the difference between distance norms of algorithms, however, an additional research on tweaking the fuzzification parameter μ could produce interesting insights about the model accuracy. It should be noted that the important factor that also needs to be accounted is integration of user profile change over the time. The self-learning algorithms that build non-deterministic models which update user privacy profile models could be a possible panacea for several issues of such recommender system. An example can be the adaptive neuro-fuzzy inference system which builds upon neural networks the knowledge base of the inference rules. The advantage of such tool against traditional inference systems is that concepts, such as people's attitudes or variables that can be explained in linguistic terms, simultaneously provide the engine for the automated prediction.

References

Bélanger, F., & Crossler, R. E. (2011). Privacy in the digital age: A review of information privacy research in information systems. *MIS Quarterly, 35*(4), 1017–1042.

Cremonesi, P., Garzotto, F., & Turrin, R. (2012). Investigating the persuasion potential of recommender systems from a quality perspective: An empirical study. *ACM Transactions on Interactive Intelligent Systems (TiiS), 2*(2), 11.

Glimcher, P. W., & Rustichini, A. (2004). Neuroeconomics: The consilience of brain and decision. *Science, 306*(5695), 447–452.

John, L. K., Acquisti, A., & Loewenstein, G. (2010). Strangers on a plane: Context-dependent willingness to divulge sensitive information. *Journal of Consumer Research, 37*(5), 858–873.

Knijnenburg, B. P., Sivakumar, S., & Wilkinson, D. (2016). Recommender systems for self-actualization. In *Proceedings of the 10th ACM Conference on Recommender Systems* (pp. 11–14). ACM.

Netter, M., Herbst, S., & Pernul, G. (2013). Interdisciplinary impact analysis of privacy in social networks. In *Security and Privacy in Social Networks* (pp. 7–26). Springer.

Smith, H. J., Dinev, T., & Xu, H. (2011). Information privacy research: An interdisciplinary review. *MIS Quarterly, 35*(4), 989–1016.

Von Alan, R. H., March, S. T., Park, J., & Ram, S. (2004). Design science in information systems research. *MIS Quarterly, 28*(1), 75–105.

Appendix A

A.1 Privacy Profiles Extraction (Fig. A.1)

#	Nombre	Tipo	Cotejamiento	Atributos	Nulo	Predeterminado	Comentarios	Extra
1	UserID	int(10)		UNSIGNED	Sí	NULL	The users.uid of the associated user.	
2	Name	varchar(60)	utf8_general_ci		No		Unique user name.	
3	Gender	varchar(255)	utf8_general_ci		Sí	NULL		
4	Birthdate	datetime			Sí	NULL		
5	MyActivity	varchar(255)	utf8mb4_general_ci		Sí	NULL		
6	ContactMe	varchar(255)	utf8mb4_general_ci		Sí	NULL		
7	MyRelations	varchar(255)	utf8mb4_general_ci		Sí	NULL		
8	MyTopics	varchar(255)	utf8mb4_general_ci		Sí	NULL		
9	PersonalInfo	varchar(255)	utf8mb4_general_ci		Sí	NULL		
10	VoteIntention	varchar(255)	utf8mb4_general_ci		Sí	NULL		

Fig. A.1 MySQL table of Participa Inteligente user privacy settings

A. Kaskina, *Citizen Privacy Framework*, Fuzzy Management Methods,
https://doi.org/10.1007/978-3-031-06021-2

Appendix B

B.1   User Evaluation Survey for Privacy Behaviour (Tables B.1 and B.2)

Table B.1 User privacy behaviour: survey questions

Number	Variable	Question	Scale
Q1	Use of default settings (actual)	Did you use the "default" privacy settings when you registered on the platform?	Yes; No
Q2	Knowledge	Did you know where and how to change the privacy options on the platform?	Yes; No
Q3	Frequency	How many times did you change privacy settings of your account?	1; 2; >2
Q4	Use of default settings (intention)	You publish all your comments and articles in "public" mode by default	Yes; No
Q5	Ease of use	The privacy options on the platform are easy to use	Totally disagree to Totally agree
Q6	Forget	Did you forget to change the privacy settings in your account?	Yes; No

Table B.2 Privacy recommendations: survey questions

Construct	Number	Question	Likert scale
Privacy behaviour consistency (PBC)	1	My privacy settings are set to public since the registration on the platform	Strongly disagree to Strongly agree
	2	I have not set up privacy settings when created an account on the platform	Strongly disagree to Strongly agree
Perceived sharpness (PSH)	3	The recommended privacy options differs from my privacy attitudes	Strongly disagree to Strongly agree
	4	The recommended privacy options are similar to my privacy attitudes	Strongly disagree to Strongly agree
	5	Recommended privacy options compromise with my privacy preferences	Strongly disagree to Strongly agree
	6	The privacy recommendations meet my privacy preferences on the platform	Strongly disagree to Strongly agree
	7	The recommendation options mismatch with my privacy preferences	Strongly disagree to Strongly agree
Perceived quality (PRQ)	8	Recommended privacy settings provide adequate protection for me	Strongly disagree to Strongly agree
	9	The recommendation gave me good privacy suggestions	Strongly disagree to Strongly agree
	10	The recommended privacy options helped me to reach my desired privacy on the platform	Strongly disagree to Strongly agree
Outcome satisfaction (OS)	11	The privacy options I saw were a waste of my time	Strongly disagree to Strongly agree
	12	I am happy with recommended to me privacy settings	Strongly disagree to Strongly agree
	13	I liked recommended privacy options	Strongly disagree to Strongly agree
	14	I am not sure if I chose the best privacy settings	Strongly disagree to Strongly agree
Reactance (RC)	15	I was influenced by the privacy recommendations provided by the system	Strongly disagree to Strongly agree
	16	I did not feel influenced by the system to select the privacy recommendation	Strongly disagree to Strongly agree
	17	I was angry with the limited freedom of choice given by the recommendations	Strongly disagree to Strongly agree
	18	I felt frustrated in my attempts to make independent privacy decision	Strongly disagree to Strongly agree
	19	I prefer to choose myself privacy settings rather than being provided with recommendation	Strongly disagree to Strongly agree

(continued)

Table B.2 (continued)

Construct	Number	Question	Likert scale
Persuasion (PS)	20	I selected privacy options recommended to me	Strongly disagree to Strongly agree
	21	I skipped privacy options recommended to me	Strongly disagree to Strongly agree
	22	I will recommend to a friend to use privacy recommendations	Strongly disagree to Strongly agree
	23	I find privacy recommendation options to be relevant	Strongly disagree to Strongly agree
	24	Privacy options were sufficient to facilitate my privacy decision	Strongly disagree to Strongly agree

Appendix C

C.1 User Evaluation Setup (Figs. C.1, C.2, and C.3)

Estimado(a) Aigul,

Reciba un saludo del equipo Participa Inteligente, una plataforma desarrollada y avalada por varias universidades del Ecuador y Europa, con el objetivo de informar a los votantes sobre los perfiles y posturas políticas de los candidatos en las pasadas elecciones de Ecuador 2017.

Queremos solicitar su colaboración para responder una encuesta en línea, cuyo objetivo es aumentar la conciencia de privacidad de los usuarios en la plataforma. Su participación no tomará más de 15 minutos y será de gran ayudará en nuestra investigación para evaluar la efectividad del soporte de privacidad personalizado que se desarrollá en la plataforma.

Para participar, por favor haga clic en el siguiente enlace:

- https://participacioninteligente.org/survey-privacy

Como agradecimiento por su participación, las primeras 100 personas que completen el cuestionario recibirán una copia del libro: **eDemocracy & eGovernment. Etapas hacia la sociedad democrática del Conocimiento, por A.Meier y L. Terán.** El libro lo podrán retirar de las instalaciones del Instituto de Altos Estudios Nacionales (IAEN).

Si tiene alguna pregunta sobre la encuesta, tiene dificultades para acceder o tiene problemas al completar la encuesta, comuníquese con aigul.kaskina@unifr.ch.

Agradecemos su colaboración.

El equipo de Participa Inteligente

Organizing Institutions:

About us? I Contact us

Fig. C.1 Screenshot of the email invitation to participate in the user study

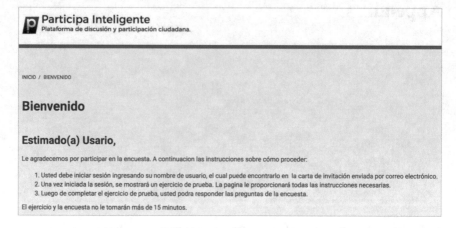

Fig. C.2 Screenshot of the evaluation application instructions

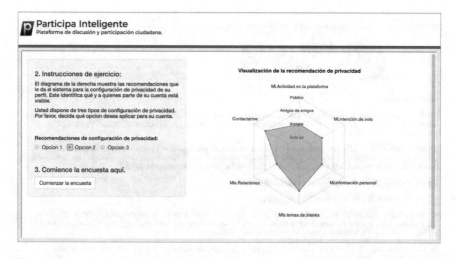

Fig. C.3 Screenshot of the exercise area for the user study

Printed in the United States
by Baker & Taylor Publisher Services